Coaching Badminton 101

Gong Chen and Carol Chen

COACHES ≡CHOICE™

ISBN: 978-1-60679-038-0
Library of Congress Control Number: 2008943334
Book layout: Studio J Art & Design
Diagrams: Gloria Hsu
Cover design: Studio J Art & Design
Front cover photo: ©Imago Sports/ZUMA Press

Coaches Choice
P.O. Box 1828
Monterey, CA 93942
www.coacheschoice.com

Dedication

To Yuan Li and Victor Chen

Acknowledgments

Special thanks to Gloria Hsu for her assistance on graphics.

Foreword

Dr. Gong Chen is one of the foremost experts on badminton in the United States. He has been intimately involved with the sport for decades, including coaching, teaching, and organizing tournaments, camps, workshops, and community programs. He has developed a reputation for his outstanding ability to instruct players from beginners to the most elite, championship-level athletes. Throughout the breadth of his experience, he has collaborated with many of the best players and coaches in the world, including notables like Dr. Li Lingwei (13-time world champion and former Olympic champion), and has incorporated their insights into this book to make it the best tool it can be. In addition, Dr. Chen has combined his knowledge and expertise as a Ph.D. in the field of kinesiology with his years of experience as a badminton player, teacher, and coach to make *Coaching Badminton 101* a unique and welcome addition to the badminton literature.

This book is the perfect tool for teaching badminton classes, coaching at the middle and high school or university level, and coaching the elite player; it also works well as a general reference for anyone seeking to improve their play or simply enjoy the game of badminton. The contents of the book are enhanced by an outstanding visual program throughout, including an extraordinary number of photographs and illustrations depicting important elements of the game (such as footwork, technique, shuttlecock trajectories, and strategic play). The book systematically covers the critical aspects of the game of badminton by logically and sequentially explaining and illustrating the critical skills of the game from etiquette and grip to the more complex components of conditioning and strategy. A unique contribution of this book is a chapter dedicated to coaching. This chapter includes sections on qualifications, organizing tournaments, and training tips for current or future coaches.

In short, Dr. Chen has compiled a systematic, thorough, readable, and, most importantly, useful tool for current or aspiring badminton players, teachers, and coaches.

Dr. Greg Payne
Acting Associate Dean of the College of Applied Sciences and Arts
San Jose State University

Dr. Greg Payne is a leading expert and book author in the discipline of motor development in the United States and the world. He is the former president of the National Association of Sport and Physical Education and the president of the California Association for Health, Physical Education, Recreation and Dance.

Contents

Preface

Coaching Badminton 101 serves as a comprehensive and practical textbook for coaching high school badminton teams and teaching beginning through advanced badminton classes in middle and high schools and universities.

I have been teaching badminton classes for more than 20 years. The contents of this book were developed based on professional badminton, university badminton, and high school badminton practice and also on my personal experience teaching beginning, intermediate, and advanced classes at the university level as well as 17 years of coaching a university badminton club, observing high school badminton practices, and coaching badminton camps with world champion and national champion players and other professional players. The contents of this book are also based on feedback from students and coaches.

The special features of this book include the following. First, it is a systematic book that covers all relevant information about badminton: skills, strategies, and training. Second, the book covers the details of all skills and strategies: grips, shuttlecock flights, hitting zones, performance, applications, returning of serves and shots, and training. Third, it uses simple terminology to describe a skill or strategy so that readers can understand the main points of badminton. Fourth, the book covers all levels of badminton for coaches and players (including middle and high school players through world champions). I consulted Dr. Li Lingwei (the top player in the world in the 1980s, a 13-time world champion and former Olympic champion, the coach of the Chinese national women's teams that were the 1999 world champions and 2000 Olympic champions, and an officer on the executive committee of the International Badminton Federation), coach Yuan Wang (retired Chinese professional and coach in the San Francisco Bay Area), university badminton instructors and students, and high school badminton coaches and players for information that makes this book applicable to high school coaches as well as instructors of university classes.

Badminton has become a popular sport in the United States, and interest in badminton is growing, especially in Southern and Northern California. Six years ago, Southern California and Northern California each had only one private badminton club. At this time, six gyms specializing in badminton only are in operation in Northern California. Community centers in these areas offer badminton classes, which are quite popular. Badminton training classes are prevalent in Northern California, and more retired badminton professionals are becoming coaches. Many high schools have badminton teams, which usually attract many students to compete for a place on the teams. This competition motivates students in middle schools and elementary schools to have early training in external classes so that they can make the team. Badminton is also popular at universities. All badminton classes offered at San Jose State University, where I am an instructor, are full every semester, and their badminton club has more than 160 members—the largest club on campus.

This book was written to help students learn to play badminton better and to enjoy badminton as a great lifetime activity. Any feedback is welcome via email at gong.chen@sjsu.edu.

—Gong Chen

1

Introduction

Present Status of Badminton in the United States

Since badminton became an Olympic sport in 1992, it has become popular in the United States. It started as a college-based sport and became a popular sport in high schools and communities.

In high schools, badminton is offered in both physical education classes and school athletic programs. Badminton is a major sport in high schools in Southern and Northern California, the areas of the United States where badminton is most popular. Spring semester is badminton season, and the season usually starts at the end of January and finishes at the beginning of June. Most school teams train on Mondays and Wednesdays and compete on Tuesdays and Thursdays. In Northern California, the official high school tournaments are run by the Central and Northern Coast Sections of the California Interscholastic Federation. Badminton is popular in high schools not only because it is fun but also because it gives athletic opportunities to students who do not compete in traditional sports such as basketball and football.

Badminton has been a popular sport in colleges and universities across the United States, and it is getting more popular as more Asian and Asian-American students enroll in college. Many universities have badminton classes in physical education departments. Badminton is also popular in the recreational and intramural sports offered evenings and weekends in open gyms on college campuses. In addition, badminton is part of athletic departments in community and junior colleges, and many colleges have badminton teams who perform in intercollegiate competitions. However, badminton is not an NCAA sport since few athletic departments sponsor it as a university sport. According to the NCAA, badminton is still an "emerging sport," and more effort is needed to promote badminton to the NCAA.

Badminton has made the most impressive progress at the community level in the United States, especially among Asian communities (including Chinese, Vietnamese, Korean, Japanese, Indian, Malaysian, and Indonesian communities). In the early 1990s, no private club or gym existed in Northern California, but by 2008 nine badminton gyms and many badminton clubs were in operation. In the early 1990s, only one or two tournaments took place in Northern California, while in 2008 a tournament occurred almost every one or two weeks. In 1993, less than 10 people signed up for a badminton tournament at a Northern California community center. Fifteen years later, similar tournaments have 150 to 300 participants. In the Chinese community in Northern California, two tournaments have taken place every June since 2003.

Badminton is also gaining momentum at the professional level in the United States. At many badminton clubs in California, athletes train and prepare for participation in tournaments. Many clubs have members who participate in national-level and national-youth-level badminton tournaments. Many clubs in California have coaches who are former professional players from China, Indonesia, and other countries where badminton is popular, helping to improve badminton training and competition levels in the United States. USA Badminton sponsors some top players who train and play in international tournaments. The training center is located in Southern California. These players usually have jobs in addition to sponsorship. USA Badminton's efforts helped the U.S. team win the men's double title in the 2005 world championship held in Anaheim, California.

Compared to players in other countries such as China, Indonesia, and Korea where the governments support professional badminton programs, the amateur players in the United States do not have enough resources for top-level professional training, which negatively impacts their skills and competition levels. Unless badminton becomes a major sport and creates a big market like basketball, the badminton competition level in the United States will not improve dramatically in the near future. Because badminton is a sport played mainly by the Asian minority population in the United States, it has a hard time competing with traditional mainstream sports, and it will take time for it to become popular at both the college level and the professional level.

Benefits

Research and practical experience have shown that playing badminton has many benefits. It benefits people of all ages, from youth to the elderly, and can be played in competitive and recreational environments. The benefits range from physical to spiritual enrichment.

Mentally and emotionally, badminton can be used to enrich people's lives. Participants can learn mental strategies that can also be applied to everyday life. Badminton training and games can help players develop mental toughness to push themselves beyond their limits or mental blocks to reach their goals. Badminton activity can help release stress in positive ways and thereby reduce a participant's chance of sickness, since 60 percent of Americans see doctors for stress-related health problems in the United States. Badminton activity also helps promote psychological well-being.

Spiritually, badminton training and games can help participants develop self-actualization through self-confidence and mental toughness. Badminton activity also helps cultivate a competitive spirit that is needed in today's competitive society.

Badminton participants can learn social rules, manners, and etiquette through training and games. Participants also learn to work and communicate with partners and opponents in the gym setting; they can use these strategies to benefit themselves in their work and life. Badminton is a friendly sport, and participants develop their manners through training and games. It is also a good sport for youth, reducing their chance of exposure to gangs and drugs.

From a practical perspective, badminton activity helps participants stay in good shape, reduce body fat, and improve body appearance and self-image. Badminton activity not only improves health-related fitness, such as muscular strength, endurance, cardiovascular endurance, and flexibility, but also improves skill-related fitness, such as explosive power, agility, speed, coordination, and hand-eye coordination. Good performance on the badminton court certainly helps improve a participant's performance at work and in everyday life. Regular badminton activity also helps to increase body metabolism.

From health and medical perspectives, badminton practice and games can help prevent muscle atrophy and osteoporosis. Badminton activity can increase high-density lipoprotein levels and lower low-density lipoprotein levels to prevent many heart-related diseases. Badminton activities can also reduce a participant's chance of diabetes, high blood pressure, cancer, bone loss, and obesity. Badminton is a great activity that helps participants develop active lifestyles for lifetime health and wellness.

Badminton Etiquette

Each sport has its own personality, out of which grows its etiquette (use of politeness) and procedures (manner of proceeding and acting). The possibility of negative feelings increases and an enjoyable atmosphere is ruined if common etiquette and procedures are not followed in a situation of playing without a referee. Badminton is a friendly sport. If a player does not follow badminton's etiquette, he will find that nobody wants to play with him, and he might lose his position in this sport. To become a skilled badminton player, you should learn to be a good player first. Following are tips to becoming a good player.

In class: When attending a badminton class, players should arrive on time and help set up the nets and poles. Players should take care of the facility and equipment, retrieve their shuttlecocks, and take down the nets and poles after class. They should respect the instructor and their classmates and avoid bad language and horseplay. Players should never walk across the court or close to the baseline or sideline when other people are practicing or playing. They should ask permission if they want to bring in someone to play.

In practice: Players should introduce themselves to partner(s) and opponent(s). They should accept latecomers. They should learn to practice with everyone in the class instead of sticking with one partner only. They should not have bias when choosing a partner since that will limit their experience and hurt other people's feelings. Players should follow the class schedule and discuss with their partners if they want to do drills that are more advanced or complicated. Players should encourage and help each other and do their best at all times.

During warm-up: Players should use half of the court for warm-ups, share the court by length, and control the bird placement in their boundary. They should warm up with their partner for double games and with opponents for single games. They should keep the bird in rally and not show off by smashing hard or tricking the practice partner. If players accidentally hit the bird into another court where other players are practicing, they should wait to retrieve the bird until those players finish the rally or stop to pick up the bird. They should ask their partner and/or opponent when they are ready to start the game.

Before the match: Players should make arrangements about the birds for the game. They should also decide on specific rules if no referee will be present. For example, they should decide if they are using old rules or new rules since both are used in local games. They should toss the bird to determine the first server and side.

During the match: Players should remember the main purpose of badminton when playing games. Enjoyment and prevention of injuries should always come before winning or losing. No point is worth winning if a player or opponent is injured or develops negative feelings. The servers should call the score and wait until their partner or opponent is ready before serving. They should call their own faults promptly, fairly, and clearly. They should also call in favor of the opponent or replay the point if they are not sure if the bird lands in or out. As a common procedure, all players should make line calls on their own side. Players should never question an opponent's call unless the opponent does not understand the rules and needs assistance.

Players should always retrieve the bird on their side. When returning the bird to the opponent for service, players should hit the bird directly to him over the net instead of shoveling it along the floor.

Players should always play their best game. Careless play is an insult to the opponent. They should always encourage their own partners and never blame the partner for making mistakes in games, since everyone makes mistakes—including world champions. Players should also compliment their opponents on their exceptionally good shots after a rally is over.

Players should follow the general rules. If a disagreement arises, they should talk it over and, if needed, play the point over. They should suggest a replay if the opponent is handicapped by an unusual interference. Emotional tantrums such as throwing rackets or using foul language have no place in the game of badminton. The customary lack of such displays is one of the reasons that badminton is attractive to players and spectators alike.

Players should shake hands with their partners and opponents, thank them for the game, and comment on the game and their play. They should be good losers and humble winners. It is also very beneficial to discuss the game with partners and opponents for feedback and suggestions.

Bad manners to avoid: Badminton players should do their best to avoid the following behaviors: lack of respect for opponents or referees; yelling, swearing, or using bad language; getting angry with people easily; throwing a racket or hitting the shuttlecock with deadly force while it is not in play; having an arrogant attitude toward an opponent; never picking up the shuttlecock and always waiting for the opponent to do it; complaining about a partner; excessive talking; arguing constantly; and laughing at other people's mistakes. Problems such as these can easily ruin a badminton career.

Common Injuries in Badminton

Although playing badminton benefits people in more than one way, players may become injured during practice or games. Players need to be aware of common injuries and their causes and know how to prevent them.

Potential injuries in badminton: Based on data and practical observation, the following injuries occur often in badminton practice and games:

- Twisted wrist muscle or tendon
- Tennis elbow
- Twisted shoulder muscle or ligament

- Twisted neck muscle
- Twisted upper-back or lower-back muscles
- Pulled hip and thigh muscles
- Sprained knee ligament
- Worn-out kneecap
- Twisted ankle muscles and ligaments
- Pulled tendon
- Shuttlecock injury on the face

Causes of injuries in badminton: Based on research and clinical observation, the following are the most common causes of injuries in badminton:
- Previous problems
- Not enough warm-ups
- Incorrect performance of techniques
- Going beyond body limits
- Too many repeated movements
- Carelessness
- Accidents
- Quick or jerky motions

Prevention of Injuries

Guidelines should be followed for the prevention of injuries. These guidelines cover a variety of factors.

Health concerns: Players should consult their physician if they have any physical problems that they feel might impact their health. Players should consult their coach or instructor about what they can do if health problems exist. Players should not play hard when they are ill or injured. They should consult the coach and do some easy drills or body conditioning.

Environment: Players should clean up the playing area before they practice or play, and the floor should be free of dust, water, and other debris. The area at least one yard from the boundary lines should be clear. Players need to be aware of the surroundings and keep out of the way of others.

Warm-up: Players should warm up for five to eight minutes before practice or play. Badminton warm-ups should include the following activities: stretching muscles and rotating joints, slow running or jumping to raise the heartbeat and warm muscles, and footwork and swinging. During a warm-up for a game, players should hit different shots with their opponent or partner. Players should wear proper attire and shoes for warm-ups and practice.

Concentration: Players should concentrate on skill development in practice and during play. They should avoid chatting when practicing or playing since it will prevent them from concentrating on their activities; lack of concentration increased the risk of injury. Players should know their own capacity and not do anything beyond their physical limit when they are not properly prepared.

Treatment of Injuries

Two types of treatment exist for sport injuries: Western and Eastern. Each treatment has its own pros and cons. The following therapeutic techniques are used in both types of treatment.

Immediate treatment: Injured players should stop practicing or playing in a game and rest immediately. They should not stretch, massage, or try to play or practice since the injury is new, even though they are still eager to play. Continuous playing after an injury will result in more and worse injuries.

Players should put ice on the injured body part to prevent or reduce the swelling. The ice should be kept in place until the swelling stops. Players should see a doctor for an examination and therapy.

Western therapy: Western therapy tends to apply ice on and compress the injured body part to reduce swelling and to stabilize the injury. Doctors also suggest that players take ibuprofen. Both ice and ibuprofen are used following injuries. For continuous treatment, Western therapy tends to apply heat and cold in combination on the injured body part and to use cortisone externally. Western doctors also use electrical stimulus to speed up the recovery. They often use stretching to release the pain and weight lifting to strengthen muscles.

Eastern therapy: Eastern therapy also uses ice to stop the swelling for acute injuries and suggests rest for injured players. Eastern doctors use herbs externally or alcohol massage to reduce swelling. When the swelling is gone, they often use acupuncture combined with therapeutic massage and electric stimulation to treat the injuries. They also use heat to speed up the blood circulation.

Comparison: Western and Eastern therapies both treat sport injuries, but their philosophies and treatment techniques differ. In Western therapy, the procedures of treating injuries are strict, and doctors follow a certain process. Eastern therapy also follows common procedures, but sometimes doctors make adjustments based on their specialties. Western medicine focuses on fixing what is broken, while Eastern medicine treats people in a holistic view and tries to treat the roots of the problem. Western medicine uses drugs to stop the pain from injuries. Eastern medicine uses herbs to stop the pain by speeding up the recovery process. Western medicine is great at treating severe injuries such as broken knees with surgeries and modern technology, while Eastern medicine effectively treats small everyday injuries such as twisted ankles and pulled muscles using acupuncture, therapeutic massage, and herbs. The effects of both therapies are individualized. Players should try both to find out which therapy works better for them.

Motivation to Play Badminton

Effective strategies exist to attract players to participate in badminton. Players should have a good understanding of the benefits of playing badminton. Coaches should make badminton fun for beginners so that they will enjoy it and want to play again. Furthermore, players need to learn proper technique and etiquette to play better and enjoy the game. The better they are, the more likely they will stay with it. Players should find a partner or group and a good place to play where they can play regularly. Players should set goals and objectives and take time from their daily schedule to practice and play games. Pretty soon, they will be aware of their achievement and the positive effects of playing badminton. Players who are not interested in competitive play can focus on enjoying the process of playing, rather than on winning the game.

2

Preparation for Training

This chapter briefly introduces proper attire and selection of equipment for badminton. Dressing properly for badminton can make movement easier and reduce the chance of injuries. Proper badminton attire (including shoes) also makes players look and feel good and shows respect to partners and opponents. Practices and competitions run much smoother with proper attire.

Attire and Equipment

Preferences for attire and equipment are individualized. However, the following attire and equipment are suggested for badminton classes, training or practice, and games. Players can use this checklist to prepare themselves after consulting with their coaches:

- Badminton shirt (Figure 2-1)
- Warm-up suit
- Badminton shoes (Figure 2-2)
- Extra shirts and socks
- Towels
- Rackets and wraps
- Nylon or feather shuttlecocks
- Tape or bandages

Figure 2-1. Badminton shirts

Figure 2-2. Badminton shoes

Equipment Selection

Rackets

Badminton rackets are manufactured by many companies (Figures 2-3 and 2-4). Famous brands include Yonex, Black Knight, Domino, Gosen, Hi-Qua, Winex, Carlton, Kason, Hi-Tec, Victor, and Yang-Yang. The prices of good rackets range from $50 to $250. Professional players usually have their own preferences for rackets, but for amateur players, most brands will work well. The criteria for choosing good rackets include the following:

- Do not go to regular stores to purchase inexpensive recreational rackets (usually around $10). Instead, go to professional dealers to purchase tournament rackets. These rackets should be one piece and made of graphite instead of metal.
- For beginners, a racket costing $50 to $80 should be fine; for intermediate and advanced players, rackets costing more than $100 better fit their games, but rackets costing $80 can still do the job.
- String tension should be sufficiently tight to ensure enough hitting power.
- Racket handles should be comfortable for the player. Players will lose control if the handle is too small, but wrist motion will be limited if the handle is too big.
- Singles players should use slightly heavier rackets for more power. Doubles players should use lighter rackets for fast shots.

Shuttlecocks (Birdies)

Shuttlecocks are manufactured by many companies as well. Therefore, different brands are sold. High school team players usually use nylon birdies for their training and competitions. The best-quality nylon shuttlecocks are Mavis birdies, which are made by Yonex (Figure 2-5). Players who participate in other tournaments usually use feather shuttlecocks (Figure 2-6). Most brands on the market are good for regular local

Figure 2-3. Racket display at a professional badminton store

Figure 2-4. Different brands of rackets

Figure 2-5. Nylon shuttlecocks

Figure 2-6. Feather shuttlecocks

tournaments if they are labeled as "tournament usage." Players usually use the same types of birdies for their regular training to get used to them, but some use less-expensive birdies for training.

Warm-Up

The warm-up is an important part of playing badminton. Warm-up activities can prevent potential injuries and prepare your body for effective practices and games. A misunderstanding exists with regard to warm-up terms and activities. People (including many coaches) tend to use the word "stretching" instead of "warm-up." This term often leads players to stretch their muscles only and forget other activities, especially those involving the joints. The joints are more vulnerable to injuries than are muscles and usually take much longer to recover if they are injured. Some joint injuries can become permanent problems and cannot be cured.

The warm-up process is individualized based on personal preferences. Each player has his own style for warm-ups. Generally, badminton warm-up should follow a pattern so that players do not skip any body part. The following four types of activities are considered a comprehensive warm-up (but the specific activities for each type of movement can be different and individualized):

- Stretching activities (to prepare all muscle groups to be used)
- Rotating activities (to prepare all involved joints)
- Running or jumping activities (to warm the muscles and raise the heart rate)
- Footwork and swinging motions

The stretching and rotation procedures can be combined together. Commonly, players start with the neck muscles and joints and then gradually go down to the ankles and toes. This activity can be done in the reverse order from the ankles to the neck. Following is an example of this type of warm-up.

- Stretch the neck to the front and back and to the shoulder (left and right) and then turn the head sideways (left and right) (Figures 2-7 to 2-12)

Figure 2-7. Forward

Figure 2-8. Backward

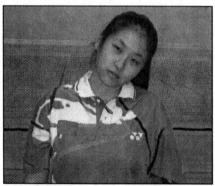

Figure 2-9. Stretch to the left shoulder

Figure 2-10. Stretch to the right shoulder

Figure 2-11. Turn to the left

Figure 2-12. Turn to the right

- Rotate shoulders in circular motions (Figures 2-13 to 2-20)

Figure 2-13. Starting position

Figure 2-14. Forward

Figure 2-15. Upward

Figure 2-16. Backward

Figure 2-17. Stretch back

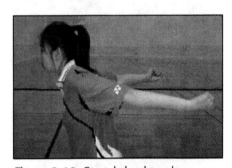

Figure 2-18. Stretch back and up

Figure 2-19. Stretch across the shoulder

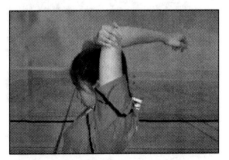

Figure 2-20. Stretch up and back

- Rotate elbows (Figures 2-21 and 2-22)

Figure 2-21. Elbow up

Figure 2-22. Elbow down

- Rotate wrists (Figures 2-23 to 2-26)

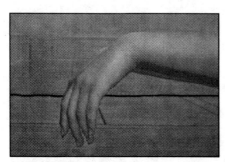

Figure 2-23. Down

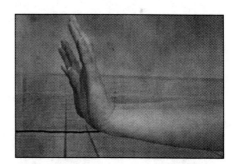

Figure 2-24. Up

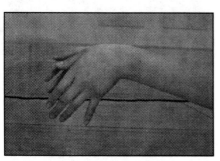

Figure 2-25. To the side and down

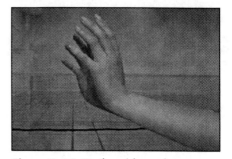

Figure 2-26. To the side and up

- Stretch upper back and lower back (Figures 2-27 to 2-32)

Figure 2-27. Turn left

Figure 2-28. Turn right

Figure 2-29. Stretch forward

Figure 2-30. Stretch back

Figure 2-31. Stretch to the left

Figure 2-32. Stretch to the right

• Rotate hip joints inward and outward (Figures 2-33 to 2-36)

Figure 2-33. Inward to the left

Figure 2-34. Inward to the right

Figure 2-35. Outward to the right

Figure 2-36. Outward to the left

- Stretch thighs (Figures 2-37 to 2-40)

Figure 2-37. Stretch the right thigh

Figure 2-38. Stretch the left thigh

Figure 2-39. Stretch one inner thigh (repeat to both sides)

Figure 2-40. Stretch both inner thighs

• Rotate knees (Figures 2-41 to 2-44)

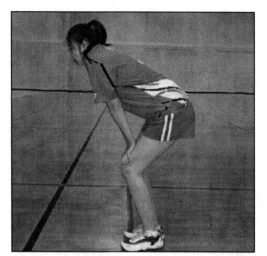

Figure 2-41. Move knees forward

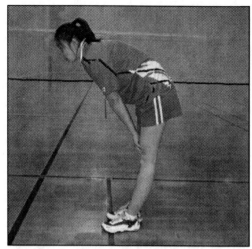

Figure 2-42. Move knees backward

Figure 2-43. Circle knees to the left

Figure 2-44. Circle knees to the right

- Stretch calf muscles (Figures 2-45 and 2-46)

Figure 2-45. Stretch the calf   Figure 2-46. Stretch the tendons

- Rotate ankles (Figure 2-47)

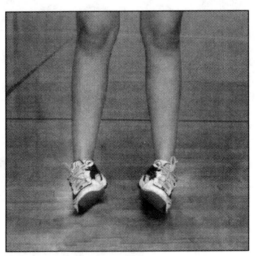

Figure 2-47. Rotate ankles

Cool-Down

Cool-down activities can reduce after-workout problems and prevent muscle tightening; these activities can also help players to quickly recover from practice and games and get them ready for the next practice or game. A cool-down process can include the following activities, which can be individualized based on personal preference. Shaking body parts can help relax tensed and tired muscles and joints. Massaging is also used by professional players for relaxation and recovery. Meditation is used by professional players not only for relaxation but also for maintaining inner health. Putting on long pants and long-sleeve sweaters after practice or games is a common practice by professional players to keep the body warm and avoid catching cold, especially in cold weather. Taking a warm shower and keeping the body clean also help players recover from practice or games.

Body Conditioning

Body conditioning is important for effective badminton playing and training and for prevention of injuries. With proper body conditioning, players can move fast, hit quickly and powerfully, and keep good form in long games with good endurance. Body conditioning is even essential to the appearance of badminton players. Badminton players usually use the racket-arm to hit the bird; therefore, it is common that their racket-arm is stronger than their other arm. Body conditioning certainly helps keep their two arms in good balance.

Body conditioning for badminton players usually includes muscle strengthening exercises especially for explosive power, endurance, speed, and agility. Muscle strength can be developed through weight lifting activities. Endurance can be improved through light weight lifting for longer periods, long distance running, and many hours of skills training and games. Agility can be enhanced through activities involving quick changes of motions and directions. Speed in badminton means footwork speed and hitting speed. Movement speed can be improved through light weight lifting with fast motion, short distance running, and zigzag running. Hitting speed can be enhanced through improving explosive power (the shoulder, arms, and wrist), efficiency of swing motion, and transition of movements.

3

Badminton Basics

This chapter introduces basic elements for badminton skills, including basic stances for serving and receiving, grips, racket motions for different shots and serves, and footwork. These basic elements are important for learning and training of badminton skills.

Grips

Two types of grips are used in badminton: the forehand grip and the backhand grip. The forehand grip is used to return shots on the forehand side (the right side if the player is right-handed), and the backhand grip is mainly used to return shots on the backhand side (the left side if the player is right-handed). Correct grips are important for learning correct skills and application of these skills in practice and games.

Forehand Grip

The forehand grip is used for all forehand shots; this grip allows for strong shots. Following are the key elements of the forehand grip:
- The left hand holds the racket; the right palm slides down to the handle, and the little finger holds the racket (Figure 3-1).
- The other fingers hold the racket loosely (Figure 3-2).
- The thumb holds the other side of the racket for a complete forehand grip (Figures 3-3 and 3-4).

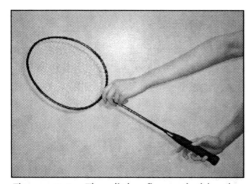

Figure 3-1. The little finger holds the handle.

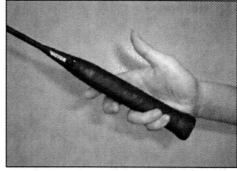

Figure 3-2. The other fingers loosely hold the handle.

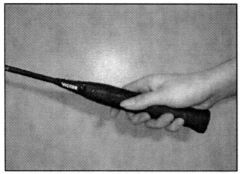

Figure 3-3. The complete forehand grip

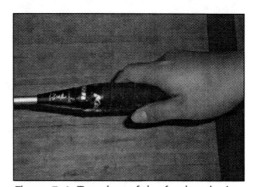

Figure 3-4. Top view of the forehand grip

Backhand Grip

The backhand grip is used for all backhand shots; backhand shots are not as strong as forehand shots. Following are the key elements of the backhand grip:

- Start from the forehand grip (Figure 3-5).
- Turn the racket face parallel to the floor (Figure 3-6) with the thumb on the top.

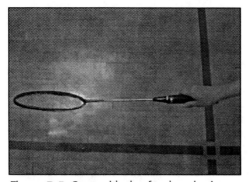

Figure 3-5. Start with the forehand grip

Figure 3-6. Turn the racket into the backhand grip

Applications

Both forehand and backhand grips are used for three types of shots. The three types of shots are underhand shots (underhand clear serve and underhand clear shot), sidearm shots (drive shot and push short), and overhead shots (overhead clear shot, overhead drop shot, and smash).

Racket Motion and Shuttlecock Flight Directions

The direction and pathway of a serve or a shot depend on how the racket contacts the shuttlecock. The racket contacts the shuttlecock in several ways, and different contacts create different flight patterns of the shuttlecock. The contacts include flat, topspin, backspin, and sidespin motions.

Flat Serves and Shots

With flat serves and shots, the racket directly hits the back of the shuttlecock perpendicularly forward, upward, or downward. The shuttlecock then travels straight forward in flat serves or shots such as drive or push shots (Figure 3-7), goes down in smash or overhead drop shots (Figure 3-8), or travels upward in clear serves, clear shots, and flick serves (Figure 3-9).

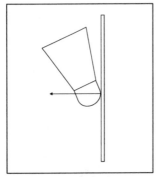
Figure 3-7. Forward

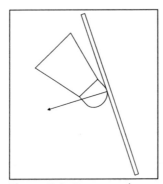
Figure 3-8. Downward

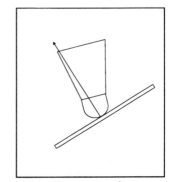
Figure 3-9. Upward

Topspin Shots

With topspin shots, the racket hits (half hit and half scratch) the low-back part of the shuttlecock bottom with an upward scratching motion. The shuttlecock then travels a little upward while forward flipping to remain low. The close net lifting drop shot usually uses this motion. The direction of a topspin shot is shown in Figure 3-10 from the side view.

Backspin Shots

With backspin shots, the racket hits (half hit and half scratch) the low part of the shuttlecock bottom with a downward-forward scratching motion. The shuttlecock travels forward with a backward spin in slice drive shots and net drop shots. Then, the shuttlecock goes up while back flipping to remain low and slows down. The direction of a backspin shot is shown in Figure 3-11 from the side view.

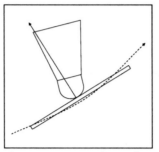

Figure 3-10. Topspin motion

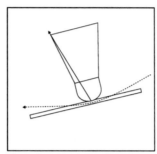

Figure 3-11. Backspin motion

Sidespin Shots

With left sidespin shots, the racket hits (half hit and half scratch) the right-back part of the shuttlecock bottom with a sideways-scratching motion for a left sidespin shot. The shuttlecock then travels toward your left-front. This motion is usually used for slice overhead drop shots and slice smashes. The shuttlecock will slow down and land on the opponent's right-front corner close to the net in drop shots or will land on the opponent's right side in smashes to confuse the opponent. The direction of a left sidespin shot is shown in Figure 3-12 from the top view.

With right sidespin shots, the racket hits (half hit and half scratch) the left-back part of the shuttlecock bottom with a sideways-scratching motion. The shuttlecock then travels toward your right-front. This motion is usually used for overhead drop shots. The shuttlecock will slow down and land on the opponent's left-front corner close to the net. The direction of a right sidespin shot is shown in Figure 3-13 from the top view.

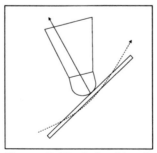

Figure 3-12. Left sidespin motion

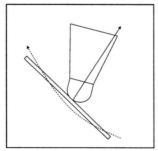

Figure 3-13. Right sidespin motion

Ready Stances

As in other sports, a ready stance in badminton is essential to movement and skills. The stances include serving stance, receiving serve stance, and basic stance in rally.

Forehand Serving Stance

All forehand serves should start with an identical stance so that the opponent does not know which serve the server is using. Forehand serves include clear, short, and drive serves. Following are the key elements of the forehand serving stance (Figure 3-14):

- The left foot is in front, and the right foot is in back.
- The left heel is up slightly with the player's body weight on the right foot.
- The left hand holds the shuttlecock up in front of the player.
- The racket is up and back with the wrist cocked.

Figure 3-14. Forehand serving stance

Backhand Serving Stance

All backhand serves should start with an identical stance so that the opponent does not know which serve the server is using. Backhand serves include flick, short, chasing, and drive serves. Following are the key elements of the backhand serving stance (Figure 3-15):

- The player's weight is on the front foot, and the back foot is on the toes with the heel up.
- The front knee and body remain straight.
- The left hand holds the shuttlecock up in front of the belly near the sweet spot of the racket.
- The right hand holds the racket with a backhand grip, and the racket head is pointing forward.

Figure 3-15. Backhand serving stance

Receiving Serve Stance

The receiving stance is the same for returning all serves in doubles and singles games. The receiver should be ready from this stance to return any serves using any skills. Following are the key elements of the receiving serve stance (Figure 3-16):
- The left foot is in front, and the right foot is back.
- The heels are up slightly, the knees are bent, and the body is slightly leaning forward.
- The left hand is in front.
- The racket is up in front with a forehand grip.
- The player watches the opponent's movement.

Figure 3-16. Receiving service stance

Basic Stance in Rally

The basic stance is the same for returning any shots in doubles and singles games. The receiver should be ready from this stance to return any shots using any skills after returning the opponent's serve. Following are the key elements of the basic stance in rally (Figure 3-17):

- Both feet are parallel to the net (the right foot can be slightly in front).
- The heels are up slightly, the knees are bent, and the body is slightly leaning forward.
- The racket is up in front, and the left hand is at the player's side naturally.
- The player watches the opponent's movement.

Figure 3-17. Basic stance in rally

Court (Center) Positions

Remaining in the proper court (also called "center") position is the first priority in badminton training and games. Most skills are used to move the opponent away from the center position and then to attack the open spots. The badminton court position is the home base, and players should return to that position immediately after a serve or shot. The center position varies in singles and doubles games.

Singles

In singles games, the center court position during rallies is in the middle of the court that the player is on (Figure 3-18). The stance is demonstrated in Figure 3-17. A player needs to go back to this position immediately after he finishes serving or receiving serve.

The server should stay in the right (Figure 3-19) or left (Figure 3-20) serving court close to the center line so that he can take one step to get into the center position with no time. The serving stance is demonstrated in Figure 3-14.

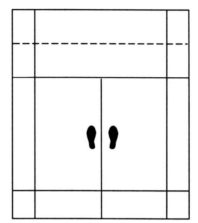

Figure 3-18. Singles center position

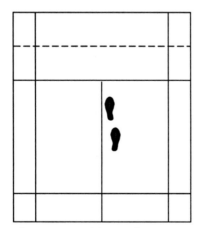

Figure 3-19. Right service

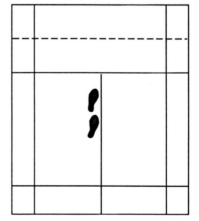

Figure 3-20. Left service

The receiver, however, usually stays toward his backhand side when receiving the serve (Figures 3-21 and 3-22) and then moves to the center position immediately after returning the serve. The receiving stance is demonstrated in Figure 3-16.

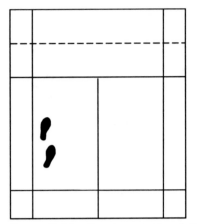

Figure 3-21. Receive at the left court

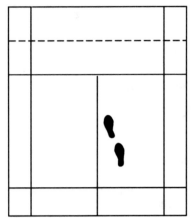

Figure 3-22. Receive at the right court

Doubles

In doubles games, the center positions for both players depend on the format the team is using at the moment—for example, side-by-side format (Figure 3-23) and front-and-back format (Figure 3-24). Both players remain in the center of the designated coverage area.

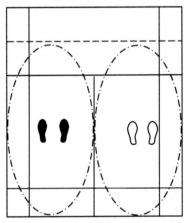

Figure 3-23. Side-by-side positions

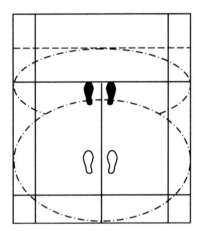

Figure 3-24. Front-back positions

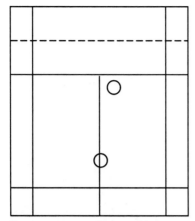

Figure 3-25. Serving position

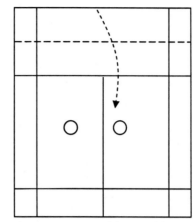

Figure 3-26. Receiving positions

In doubles serving positions, the server should stay in the corner of the front service line and the center line (Figure 3-25), while the partner strides on the center line. Doubles receiving positions are demonstrated in Figure 3-26, with the receiver standing on the backhand side and the receiver's partner staying in the middle of his side.

Footwork

Footwork is important in badminton. To make effective shots, a player must move and position himself properly before hitting the shuttlecock. Six directions of footwork follow. All footwork requires that the heel lands first.

Toward the Right-Front

Two kinds of footwork are used to move toward the right-front. One type uses two steps (Figures 3-27 to 3-30), and the other type uses three steps (Figures 3-31 to 3-35), depending on the player's stance and preference. The returning footwork is the same (Figure 3-36).

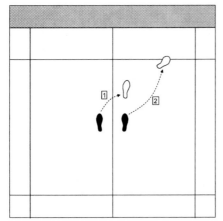

Figure 3-27. Two steps to the right-front

Figure 3-28. Basic stance

Figure 3-29. Left step

Figure 3-30. Right step

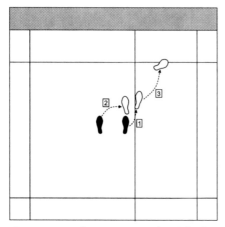

Figure 3-31. Three steps to the right-front

Figure 3-32. Basic stance

Figure 3-33. Right step

Figure 3-34. Left step cross or follow right step

Figure 3-35. Right step

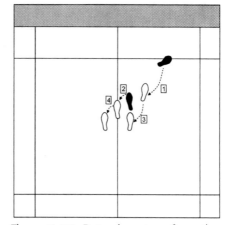

Figure 3-36. Returning steps from the right-front

Toward the Left-Front

Two kinds of footwork are used to move toward the left-front. One type uses two steps (Figures 3-37 to 3-40), and the other uses three steps (Figures 3-41 to 3-45), depending on the player's stance and preference. The returning footwork is the same for both (Figure 3-46).

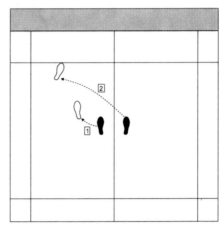

Figure 3-37. Two steps to the left-front

Figure 3-38. Basic stance

Figure 3-39. Left step

Figure 3-40. Right step

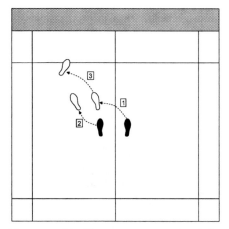

Figure 3-41. Three steps to the left-front

Figure 3-42. Basic stance

Figure 3-43. Right step

Figure 3-44. Left step

Figure 3-45. Right step

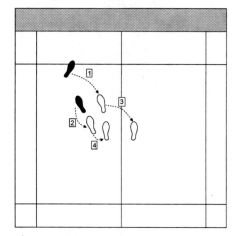

Figure 3-46. Returning

Toward the Right Side

Two kinds of footwork are used to move to the right side. The one-step footwork to the right side is demonstrated in Figures 3-47 to 3-49, and the returning footwork is demonstrated in Figure 3-50. The two-step footwork to the right side is shown in Figures 3-51 to 3-54. The returning footwork is shown in Figure 3-55.

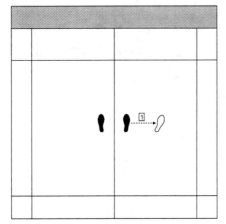

Figure 3-47. One step to the right

Figure 3-48. Basic stance

Figure 3-49. Right step to the side

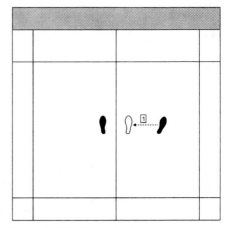

Figure 3-50. Returning step

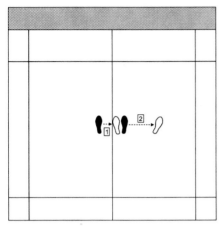

Figure 3-51. Two steps to the right

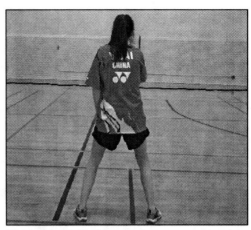

Figure 3-52. Basic stance

Figure 3-53. Left step toward the right foot

Figure 3-54. Right step to the right

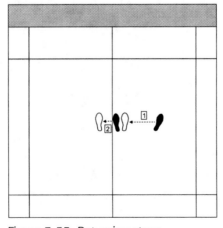

Figure 3-55. Returning steps

Toward the Left Side

One kind of footwork is used to move to the left side. The two-step footwork to the left side is demonstrated in Figures 3-56 to 3-59, and the returning footwork is shown in Figure 3-60.

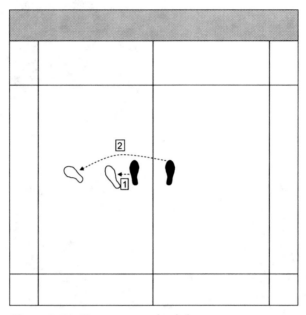

Figure 3-56. Two steps to the left

Figure 3-57. Basic stance

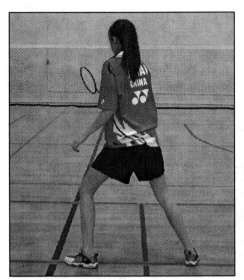
Figure 3-58. Left step

Figure 3-59. Right step

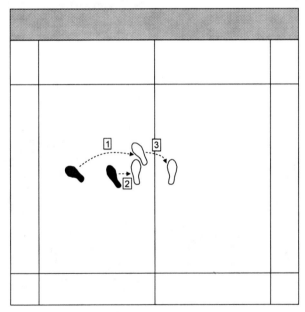
Figure 3-60. Returning

Toward the Right-Back

The footwork used to move to the right-back is common from the center position (Figures 3-61 to 3-69). The returning footwork is demonstrated in Figure 3-70. In other situations, small-step footwork, sliding, or jumping steps are also used, although not as often.

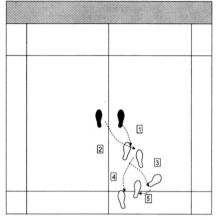

Figure 3-61. Footwork to the right-back

Figure 3-62. Basic stance

Figure 3-63. Right step

Figure 3-64. Left step

Figure 3-65. Right step

Figure 3-66. The right foot is ready to jump

Figure 3-67. The left foot moves backward

Figure 3-68. Rotate to the left and hit

Figure 3-69. Follow through to the left

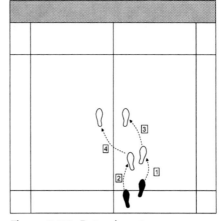

Figure 3-70. Returning steps

Toward the Left-Back

Two common footwork steps are used to move toward the left-back. One is for backhand shots (Figures 3-71 to 3-76) and returning (Figure 3-77). The other one is for forehand or around-the-head shots (Figures 3-78 to 3-85), and the returning step is demonstrated in Figure 3-86.

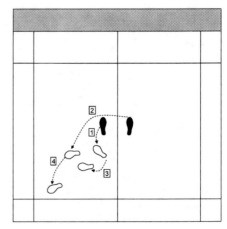

Figure 3-71. Footwork to the left-back for backhand shots

Figure 3-72. Basic stance

Figure 3-73. Left step

Figure 3-74. Right step

Figure 3-75. Left step

Figure 3-76. Right step and hit

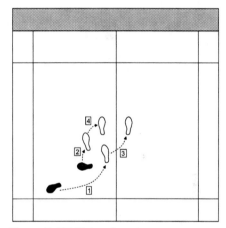

Figure 3-77. Returning steps

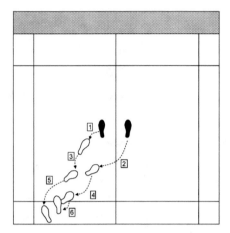

Figure 3-78. Footwork to the left-back for forehand shots

Figure 3-79. Basic stance

Figure 3-80. Left step

Figure 3-81. Right step

Figure 3-82. Left step cross

Figure 3-83. The right foot is ready to jump

Figure 3-84. The right foot jumps, and swing back.

Figure 3-85. Hit and rotate to the left

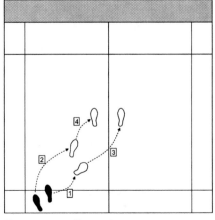

Figure 3-86. Returning steps

Shuttlecock-Handling Exercises

Shuttlecock-handling exercises are used to improve shuttlecock-handling ability and can be done individually. Beginning players should perform these activities as much as they can to get familiar with the racket and handling the shuttlecock. Intermediate and advanced players can improve too by practicing alone since many underhand clear, drive, overhead clear, and smash shots and even combination drills can be done on a wall.

Hitting Up

Using a forehand or backhand grip, hit the bird two to three yards high continuously to learn how to control the shuttlecock with arm and wrist motions. When you can handle the bird well, you can hit it up toward the ceiling to feel full power. Forehand hitting up is demonstrated in Figures 3-87 to 3-89, and backhand hitting up is shown in Figures 3-90 to 3-92.

Figure 3-87. Start with the wrist bent

Figure 3-88. Hit the bird up

Figure 3-89. Follow through

Figure 3-90. Swing back

Figure 3-91. Hit the bird up

Figure 3-92. Follow through

Wall Underhand Shots

Using a forehand or backhand grip, hit the bird forward and upward like hitting underhand clear shots to learn how to control and return a wall underhand shot. Forehand hitting up is demonstrated in Figures 3-93 to 3-95, and backhand hitting up is shown in Figures 3-96 to 3-98.

Figure 3-93. Swing back with the wrist bent

Figure 3-94. Contact

Figure 3-95. Follow through

Figure 3-96. Swing back

Figure 3-97. Contact

Figure 3-98. Follow through

Wall Overhead Shot

Using a forehand or backhand grip, hit the bird up with overhead clear shots. You can work on forehand or backhand shots or even combination skills. Figures 3-99 to 3-101 demonstrate the wall overhead shot.

Figure 3-99. Preparation

Figure 3-100. Contact

Figure 3-101. Follow through

Wall Drive Shot

Using a forehand or backhand grip, hit the shuttlecock flat directly toward the wall continuously with a forehand or backhand shot or alternatively. This motion is the same that used in the forehand drive shot (Figures 3-102 to 3-104) and the backhand drive shot.

Figure 3-102. Swing back

Figure 3-103. Contact

Figure 3-104. Follow through

Footwork Training

Following are tips for footwork training for players:
- Practice each of the six types of footwork.
- Move to all six directions and come back to the center position every time.
- Follow partner's pointing to different directions with proper and fast footwork.
- Mirror with a fast player on the other side of the net and then move with your partner.
- Put several shuttlecocks at the six spots on the sidelines; move to each spot, pick up one shuttlecock, and move to a different spot to put it down.
- Use drills that require footwork to work on both applied footwork and skills, including "clear shot-drop shot-drop shot-drop shot," "clear clear drop drop," and "clear smash-drop."

4

Serves and Returns

This chapter introduces different services, applications, and returns in badminton. Badminton services can be classified into forehand and backhand serves, high and low serves, and long and short serves. The four basic badminton serves are clear serves, drive serves, short serves, and flick serves. Clear serves, drive serves, and forehand short serves are usually used in singles games. Short serves and flick serves are usually used in doubles games. The purposes, functions, performance, applications, and returns for the four badminton serves are reviewed.

Clear Serves

The clear serve is the basic badminton serve, and all other serves are easy to learn after learning the clear serve. The clear serve is also one of the two most important skills in badminton (the other is the overhead clear shot). After learning the clear serve, a player can practice more with partners, and learning will be easier. Two clear serves exist: the defensive serve (which is high and safe) and the offensive serve (which is low and fast but is easier to hit out of bounds).

Purposes:
- Drive opponents to the backcourt so they will not smash hard.
- Force a weak return.
- Get the shuttlecock behind opponents fast (offensive).

Applications:
- As the major serve for singles games.
- To opponents who are not very strong at the backcourt.
- To opponents who tend to stay in front.
- To opponents who cannot smash at the backcourt.

Pathway: As shown in Figure 4-1, the defensive clear serve flies high and falls vertically (#1), the offensive clear serve flies lower but faster (#2), and both serves land between the doubles service line and back boundary line.

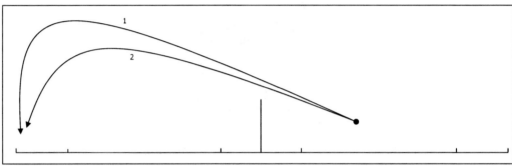

Figure 4-1. Pathways of defensive and offensive clear serves

Performance:
- Take the forehand serving stance (Figure 4-2).
- Shift body weight forward and drop the shuttlecock (Figure 4-3).
- Swing downward, forward, and then upward and hit the shuttlecock at the right-front with wrist snapping fast (Figure 4-4).
- Rotate body to the left and follow through with the racket over the left shoulder (Figure 4-5).
- Hit forward more in an offensive serve; hit higher in a defensive serve.

Figure 4-2. Serving stance

Figure 4-3. Drop and swing back

Figure 4-4. Contact at the right-front

Figure 4-5. Follow through

Returning clear serves (Figure 4-6):

- Use overhead drop shot to the two front-court corners (#1).
- Smash at the sides if the serve is short (#2).
- Use overhead clear shot to the backhand corner and alternately to the forehand corner (#3).

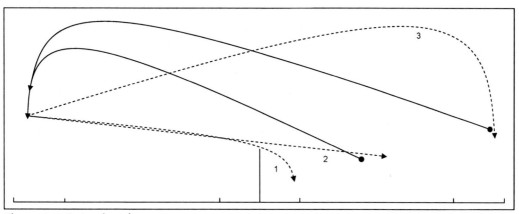
Figure 4-6. Returning clear serves

Tactics:

- Keep the serve deep.
- Serve to corners alternately.
- Make the motion identical to that of other serves.
- Alternate defensive and offensive serves to confuse opponents.
- Use alternately with drive or short serves.

Drive Serves

The drive serve is not used as often as the clear serve, but it can be used to surprise opponents, catching them off guard. The drive serve flies flat but is fast and long, and it targets the back inside corners in singles games. Alternately using the drive serve with clear and short serves can confuse opponents and force mistakes and weak returns.

Purposes:
- Drive the opponent to the backcourt by surprise.
- Get the bird to the open back corners as fast as possible.
- Catch opponents off guard and force weak returns or mistakes.
- Make opponents less aggressive.

Applications:
- To opponents who tend to stay in front.
- To opponents who have slow reactions.
- To opponents who cannot return such serves.
- To opponents who leave openings at the inside corners.

Pathway: The drive serve flies flat but fast and goes to the corner closer to the center line between the doubles service line and the back boundary line. The flight of a drive serve is shown in Figure 4-7, and the targets are shown in Figure 4-8.

Performance:

The forehand drive serve is performed as follows:
- Take the forehand serving stance (Figure 4-9).
- Drop the shuttlecock and shift body weight forward (Figure 4-10).
- Swing downward and then forward and hit the shuttlecock at the right-front fast and flat forward (Figure 4-11).
- Rotate body to the left and follow through with the racket to the left shoulder (Figure 4-12).

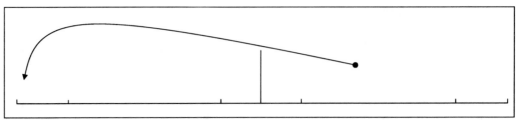

Figure 4-7. Drive serve pathway

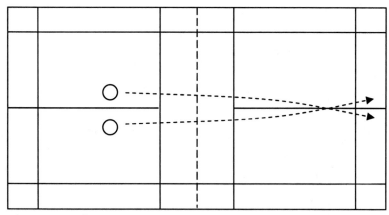

Figure 4-8. Drive serve target

Figure 4-9. Basic stance

Figure 4-10. Drop and swing back

Figure 4-11. Contact fast and forward

Figure 4-12. Follow through

The backhand drive serve is performed as follows:
- Take the backhand serving stance with the shuttlecock far in front (Figure 4-13).
- Swing back and swing forward fast (Figure 4-14).
- Hit the shuttlecock off the left hand (Figure 4-15).
- Follow through further forward (Figure 4-16).

Figure 4-13. Serving stance

Figure 4-14. Swing back

Figure 4-15. Snap fast at contact

Figure 4-16. Follow through forward

Returning drive serves (Figure 4-17):
- Block or drop shot angles (#1) to keep the serve down or if you are not ready.
- Clear back upward (#2) if the opponent is rushing forward.

Tactics:
- Keep the serve deep and fast to the openings.
- Hit to the corners and the opponent's chest alternately.

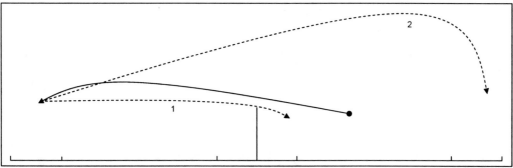

Figure 4-17. Returning drive serves

- Make motion identical to that of other serves.
- Use alternately with clear or short serves.

Short Serves

The short serve flies low and short, targeting the two front corners in singles games as well as in doubles games. Short serves make it impossible for opponents to return aggressively. Alternately using short serves with clear and drive serves in singles games and with flick serves in doubles games can confuse opponents and force mistakes and weak returns.

Purposes:
- Keep the serve low to avoid aggressive returns.
- Force opponents to lift up so that you can attack.

Applications:
- To opponents who are aggressive at high serves.
- To opponents who are not good at net play.
- For servers who play the net well.
- To move opponents back and forth.

Pathway (Figure 4-18): The short serve flies just over the top of the net, remains low, and goes to the inside or outside corners.

Performance:

The forehand short serve is performed in a manner similar to that of forehand clear and drive serves. The forehand short serve is used more in singles with clear and drive serves.

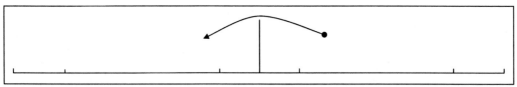

Figure 4-18. Short serve pathway

- Take the forehand serving stance (Figure 4-19).
- Drop the shuttlecock and shift body weight forward (Figure 4-20).
- Swing downward and then forward and contact the shuttlecock at the right-front with slow and controlled motion (Figure 4-21).
- Rotate body to the left and follow through with the racket to the left-front (Figure 4-22).

Figure 4-19. Serving stance

Figure 4-20. Drop and swing back

Figure 4-21. Contact

Figure 4-22. Follow through

The backhand short serve is performed in a manner similar to that of backhand drive serves but with less power. It is usually used in doubles games. However, in the 2008 Summer Olympic Games, backhand short serves were mostly used in men's single games, while traditional clear serves were rarely used.

- Take the backhand serving stance (Figure 4-23).
- Swing back (Figure 4-24).
- Hit the shuttlecock off the left hand with good control (Figure 4-25).
- Follow through further forward (Figure 4-26).

Figure 4-23. Serving stance

Figure 4-24. Swing back

Figure 4-25. Swing and contact

Figure 4-26. Follow through

Returning short serves (Figure 4-27):
- Net drop shot if the serve is low (#1).
- Rush the serve if it is high (#2).
- Push shot to the back two corners to force weak returns (#3).
- Clear shot to the back corners if opponents are not aggressive (#4).

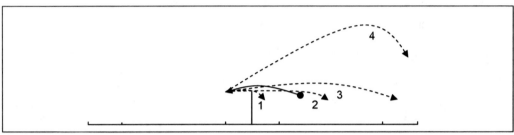

Figure 4-27. Returning short serves

Tactics:
- Keep the serve low and short.
- Go to corners alternately.
- Make motion identical to that of other serves and use alternately with clear, drive, or flick serves.
- Target at openings and watch opponent's movement.

Flick Serves

The flick serve is used only in doubles games together with short serves. The flick serve flies either fast and flat to the inside back corners or fast and high to the outside corners. Alternately using flick serves with short serves can confuse opponents and force mistakes and weak returns.

Purposes:
- Catch opponents off guard to force mistakes by getting the bird behind them as fast as possible.
- Drive opponents to the backcourt corner to score or to force a weak return.
- Confuse opponents when used with short serves.

Applications:
- One of the two serves used in doubles games.
- To opponents who are crawling the net.

- Alternately used with short serves to keep opponents guessing.
- To opponents who do not know how to return such serves.

Pathway (Figure 4-28): The flick serve can be classified as a high serve or a low serve. The high serve (#1) flies over the receiver's racket and lands at the outside corner (or the inside corner). The low serve (#2) is more like a short drive short, going either to the inside corners or toward the receiver's chest.

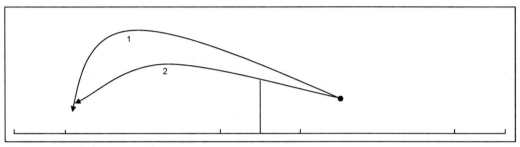

Figure 4-28. Flick serve pathways

Performance:

The forehand flick serve is performed as follows:
- Take the forehand serving stance (Figure 4-29).
- Drop the shuttlecock and shift body weight forward (Figure 4-30).
- Hit upward for a high serve but forward for a low serve (Figure 4-31).
- Hit the shuttlecock with a quick motion on contact (Figure 4-31).
- Rotate body to the left and follow through with the racket to the left front (Figure 4-32).

Figure 4-29. Serving stance

Figure 4-30. Drop and swing back

Figure 4-31. Contact easily

Figure 4-32. Follow through

The backhand flick serve is performed as follows:
- Take the backhand serving stance (Figure 4-33).
- Swing back and swing forward fast with good control (Figure 4-34).
- Hit the shuttlecock off the hand with quick elbow and wrist motions (Figure 4-35).
- Hit upward for a high serve but forward for a low serve and follow through (Figure 4-36).

Figure 4-33. Serving stance

Figure 4-34. Swing back

Figure 4-35. Contact

Figure 4-36. Follow through

Returning flick serves (Figure 4-37):
- Drop or block if no time exists for a good return or the server steps back (#1).
- Smash if the receiver is in a good position (#2).
- Clear shot back as a safe return and go back to the center position (#3).

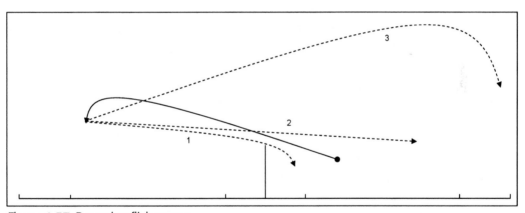

Figure 4-37. Returning flick serves

Tactics:
- Keep the serve high enough and fast.
- Go to corners alternately.
- Make motion identical to that of other serves and alternate with other serves.
- Target at openings and watch opponent's movement.

Training for Serves

Drills for Serves

The following drills are effective at developing players' skills. Coaches can choose drills depending on their players' needs.

Step #1: Feel the motion and acquire the correct form for each serve.

- Practice the same serve over and over with multiple shuttlecocks.
- Serve with a partner back and forth and provide feedback on placement.
- Perform the swing in front of a mirror and compare it with teacher's motion.
- Videotape serves and get feedback from the teacher.

Step #2: Work on the consistency of serves.

- Serve as much as possible toward opponent's forehand and backhand sides.
- Serve from left and right sides.

Step #3: Work on placements and changing lines of forehand and backhand sides.

- Serve from the left court alternately toward opponent's forehand and backhand sides.
- Serve from the right court alternately toward opponent's forehand and backhand sides.

Step #4: Alternate different serves with identical motions.

- Alternate defensive and offensive clear serves for singles games.
- Alternate clear serve, short serve, and drive serve for singles games.
- Alternate short serve and flick serve for doubles games.

Step #5: Serve with a partner returning all serves.

- Use each serve and see how effective it is from partner's returns.
- Alternate serves and see how effective it is from partner's returns.
- Use each serve and then return partner's shot.

Step #6: Serve in games.

- Use each serve in games to check the effectiveness and identify problems.
- Alternate different serves in games and get feedback and experience.

Drills for Receiving Serves and Shots

Practice of receiving serves can follow the same steps used in serving. Following is a simple format for these drills, which are effective at developing players' receiving skills and experience:

- Return each serve with one skill to one target for consistency and placement.
- Return each serve with different skills to different targets for control.
- Return serves from your partner who alternately performs different serves in a singles game format (clear, drive, and short serves).
- Return serves from your partner who alternately performs different serves in a doubles game format (short and flick serves).
- Play games and return different serves for feedback and experience. Work on weaknesses during the next training session.

5

Underhand Clear Shot

The underhand clear shot functions the same as the clear serve, and it is an important skill in badminton for practice and games. After learning this shot, a player can practice more with a partner, and learning badminton will be easier. Performing an underhand clear shot is almost the same as performing the clear serve except that the right foot steps forward as the last step but with a smaller backswing motion. Players can use either the forehand grip or the backhand grip for underhand clear shots.

Skills and Applications

Purposes:
- Drive opponents to the backcourt.
- Force weak returns or mistakes.
- Return drop shots and smashes.

Applications:
- To opponents who are not very strong at the backcourt.
- To opponents who tend to stay in front.
- To opponents who cannot smash at the backcourt.
- When opponents are moving forward.
- To make opponents tired if they smash too much.
- Returning drop shots and smashes.

Pathway (Figure 5-1): The underhand clear shot flies high, falls vertically, and lands between the doubles service line and the back boundary line.

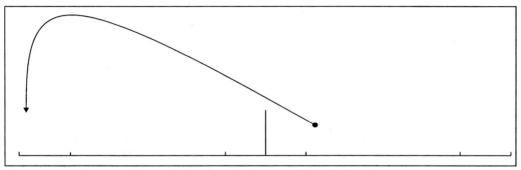

Figure 5-1. Pathway of the underhand clear shot

Performance:

The forehand underhand clear shot is performed as follows:

- From the rally stance (Figure 5-2).
- The right foot steps forward while swinging back (Figure 5-3).
- Swing forward and upward with the wrist snapping fast (Figure 5-4).
- The racket follows through to the left (Figure 5-5).

Figure 5-2. Rally stance

Figure 5-3. Step forward and swing back

Figure 5-4. Contact at the right-front

Figure 5-5. Snap and follow through to the left

The backhand underhand clear shot is performed as follows:
- From the rally stance (Figure 5-6).
- The right foot steps forward while swinging back (Figure 5-7).
- Swing forward and upward with the wrist snapping fast (Figure 5-8).
- The racket follows through to the right (Figure 5-9).

Figure 5-6. Rally stance

Figure 5-7. Step forward and swing back

Figure 5-8. Contact

Figure 5-9. Follow through to the right

Returning underhand clear shots: Refer to the instructions for returning clear serves in Chapter 4.

Tactics:
- Keep the shots deep and alternate to corners.
- Make the performance identical to that of drop and push shots and use alternately with push and drop shots.

Training for the Underhand Clear Shot

The following drills are useful in the development of players' underhand clear shots. Coaches and players can select drills based on their specific needs.

- The partner tosses, hits, or serves the bird to the forehand side, and the player uses a forehand grip to return it with an underhand clear shot.

- The partner tosses, hits, or serves the bird to the backhand side, and the player uses a backhand grip to return it with an underhand clear shot.

- The partner tosses, hits, or serves the bird to the forehand and backhand sides alternately, and the player uses forehand and backhand underhand clear shots accordingly to different corners.

- The partner uses an overhead drop shot while the player feeds with underhand clear shots to the forehand and/or backhand side based on the circumstance (Figures 5-10 and 5-11). This drill allows players to work on consistency and placement of forehand and backhand underhand clear shots, forehand (around-the-head) and backhand overhead drop shots, and slice overhead drop shots. Players can also change lines for dropping and returning, as shown in Figure 5-10.

- The partner tosses, hits, or serves the bird to the forehand and backhand sides, and the player alternates underhand clear shots and net drop shots to work on changing skills.

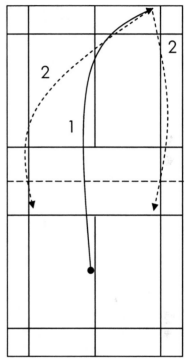

Figure 5-10. Top view of the clear-drop drill

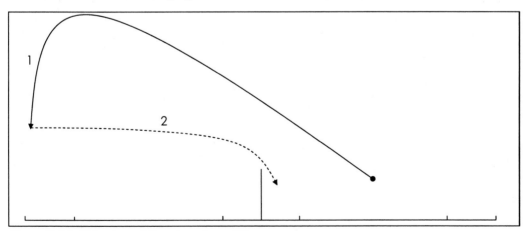

Figure 5-11. Side view of the clear-drop drill

6

Overhead Clear Shot

The overhead clear shot is another important skill in badminton together with the clear serve and the underhand clear shot. The overhead clear shot is the basis for all other overhead shots, and these two skills are needed to play badminton. Without decent clear shots, it is impossible to play badminton effectively.

Clear shots can be classified as forehand, backhand, and around-the-head clear shots. The forehand clear shot is used to return a shot on the forehand side with the forehand grip. The around-the-head shot is used to return shots on the backhand side with the forehand grip and motion. The backhand clear shot is used to return shots on the backhand side with the backhand grip. Around-the-head and backhand shots have the same function of returning shots on the backhand side. The forehand clear shot is the strongest shot in badminton followed by the around-the-head clear shot; therefore, these two shots should be used most of the time. The backhand clear shot is the weakest shot in badminton and should be used only when the forehand shot or the around-the-head clear shot cannot be used.

Overhead clear shots also include defensive clear and offensive clear shots. The defensive clear shot flies high and gives a player more time to get back to the center position while forcing an opponent to move back in a less aggressive manner. The offensive clear shot is used to quickly place the birdie behind the opponent, giving him no time for a strong return.

Skills and Applications

Purposes:

- Drive opponents to the backcourt so that they will not smash hard.
- Quickly get the bird behind opponents in offensive clear shots.
- Create time for the player to come back to the center position.
- Force weak returns.

Applications:

- To opponents who are not very strong at the backcourt.
- To opponents who tend to stay in front.
- To opponents who cannot smash at the backcourt.
- To opponents who cannot move back fast.
- Mainly used to return clear serves, clear shots, and high flick serves.

Pathway (Figure 6-1): The defensive clear shot (#1) flies high and deep, falling vertically near the single back line. The offensive clear shot (#2) flies flatter but faster, getting the bird behind the opponent quickly. The offensive clear shot is also called the "attacking clear shot."

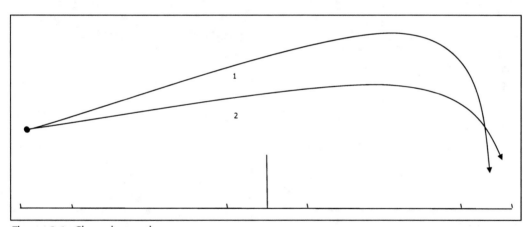

Figure 6-1. Clear shot pathways

Performance:

The forehand clear shot is performed as follows:

- Start with the basic stance and move into position (Figure 6-2).
- Jump off from the right foot, turn the body to the left, and swing the left foot back (Figure 6-3).
- Use full belly power and shoulder power to swing forward and hit the bird at the up-front of the right shoulder, with the elbow leading and the wrist snapping fast (Figure 6-4).
- Land with the left foot first at the back and follow through (Figure 6-5).

Figure 6-2. Move into position and get ready

Figure 6-3. Ready to jump and rotate

Figure 6-4. Contact

Figure 6-5. Follow through

The around-the-head clear shot (Figure 6-6) is similar to the forehand clear shot. The whole motion is the same except that the hitting zone of the around-the-head clear shot is located at the front of the left shoulder.

Figure 6-6. Around-the-head clear shot

The backhand clear shot is performed as follows:
- Start with the last step of the backhand footwork.
- The right foot takes the last step with the back toward the opponent; swing back toward the left across the body (Figure 6-7).
- Rotate the trunk and the right shoulder back fast, with the elbow leading the racket to swing at the bird with full power; contact the bird at the up-back of the shoulder with the wrist snapping (Figure 6-8).

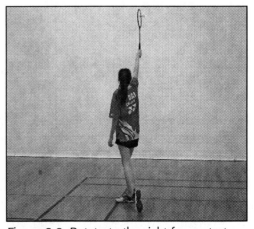

Figure 6-7. Rotate to the left and swing back   Figure 6-8. Rotate to the right for contact

Returning clear shots (Figure 6-9):
- Overhead drop shot to the two front-court corners (#1).
- Smash at the sides if the shot is short (#2).
- Overhead clear shot to the backhand or forehand corners (#3).
- Drive back if it is too late and the bird is below your head.

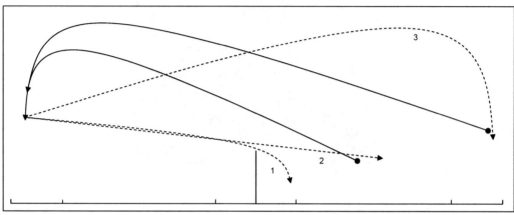

Figure 6-9. Returning clear shots (serves)

Tactics:
- Keep the shots deep and hit to the two back corners alternately.
- Clear shot back to the opponent's backhand corner whenever possible.
- Make the motion identical to that of drop and smash shots and alternately use drop and clear shots.
- Use offensive clear shots to force weak returns.
- Use defensive clear shots to get back to the center position.
- Attack if the returning shot is short.

Training for the Overhead Clear Shot

The training drills for the overhead clear shot are easy; they are designed based on game situations to a certain degree. These drills will help players acquire skills and improve consistency, placement, and speed and power of skills.
- Feed-clear shot drill:
    - ✓The partner feeds with a clear serve, and the player uses forehand, around-the-head, and backhand clear shots to one corner for consistency and placement.
    - ✓The player hits to two corners to work on changing lines.

✓The partner feeds shots to different corners, and the player returns with forehand, around-the-head, or backhand clear shots to work on judgment, movement, and use of proper shots.

• Clear shot rally drill (Figures 6-10 and 6-11): Players can work on consistency and placement of defensive clear shots, offensive clear shots, forehand and around-the-head clear shots, and backhand clear shots. Players also can change lines (crosscourt or down-the-line).

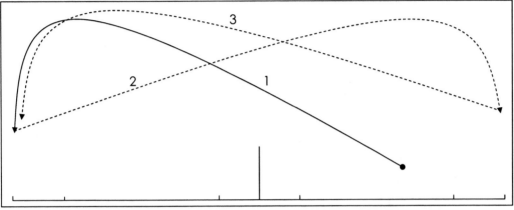

Figure 6-10. Side view of the clear shot rally drill

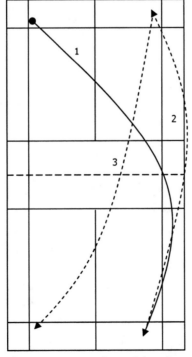

Figure 6-11. Top view of the clear shot rally drill

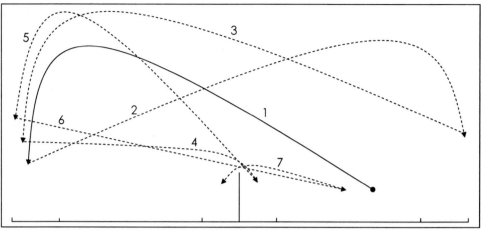

Figure 6-12. Side view of the backcourt combination drill

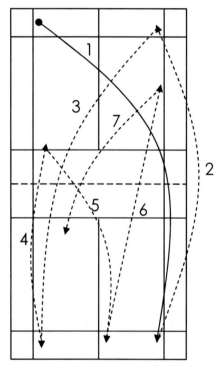

Figure 6-13. Top view of the backcourt combination drill

- Backcourt combination drill (Figures 6-12 and 6-13): The partner feeds only with clear (underhand or overhead) shots, and the player alternates clear, drop, and smash shots with identical motion. Training for clear shots should be done together with other skills so that players can hit different shots with identical motion to fake out opponents. This drill is useful after the player has learned all three required skills (overhead clear, overhead drop, and smash shots). The backcourt combination drill is also called the "clear-clear-clear-drop-clear-smash-drop" drill. This drill includes seven shots (underhand clear, overhead clear, overhead clear, overhead drop, underhand clear, smash, and block shots). The purpose of this drill is to improve the performance of overhead clear, overhead drop, and smash shots alternately with identical motion. It also works on the partner's return of these three shots. After the player masters the drill, he should use clear, drop, and smash shots randomly instead of following the same pattern.

7

Overhead Drop Shot

The overhead drop shot is an important badminton skill, and it works effectively in combination with clear shots to move opponents back and forth. The overhead drop shot is mainly used to hit the bird close to the net so that opponents cannot move fast enough to return it; this shot is also used to move opponents forward, and then the clear shot is used to move opponents back so that they tire out and make mistakes. Performing the overhead drop shot is almost exactly the same as performing the overhead clear shot, except that the hitting zone of the drop shot is much farther in front of the shoulder than that of the clear shot and less power is used.

Overhead drop shots can be classified as forehand, around-the-head, and backhand drop shots. The forehand drop shot is used to return shots on the forehand side with the forehand grip. The around-the-head drop shot is used to return shots on the backhand side with the forehand grip and motion. The backhand drop shot is used to return shots on the backhand side with the backhand grip, especially when the shot is below the shoulder level. Around-the-head and backhand drop shots return shots on the backhand side.

Forehand overhead drop shots include flat and slice (i.e., left-spin and right-spin) drop shots. The flat drop shot is the basic drop shot; it has more control but tends to drop long, making it easy for opponents to return. In the flat drop shot, the racket should be facing the opponent, and the shuttlecock is hit flat forward. Slice drop shots fly toward the right or left and fall closer to the net. The racket motion is either left spin or right spin, with the racket pointing halfway to the side.

Skills and Applications

Purposes:
- Catch openings when opponents are back and force weak returns.
- Force opponents to lift up and then attack.
- Force opponents to play the net if they are not good at net play.
- Move opponents back and forth by combining with clear shots.

Applications:
- When opponents are far back.
- When opponents are at the back and move slowly.
- When opponents are not good at net play.
- When opponents are moving toward the backcourt.

Pathway (Figure 7-1): The overhead drop shot comes down close to the net and lands between the net and the front service line.

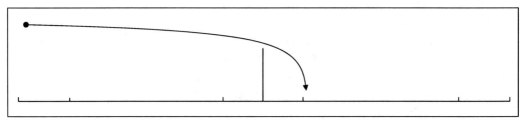

Figure 7-1. Overhead drop shot pathway

Performance:

The flat forehand overhead drop shot is performed as follows:
- Start with the basic stance and move into position (Figure 7-2).
- Jump off from the right foot, turn the body to the left, and swing left foot back (Figure 7-3).
- Swing forward and contact the birdie at the far front of the right shoulder, with the elbow leading and the wrist snapping fast (Figure 7-4).
- Land with the left foot first at the back and follow through (Figure 7-5).

Figure 7-2. Move into position and be ready

Figure 7-3. Ready to jump and rotate

Figure 7-4. Contact far in front of the right shoulder

Figure 7-5. Follow through

The around-the-head drop shot (Figure 7-6) is similar to the forehand overhead drop shot. The whole motion is the same except that the hitting zone of the around-the-head drop shot is located at the front of the left shoulder.

Figure 7-6. Around-the-head drop shot

The left slice drop shot is similar to the flat drop shot except for the moment of contact, when the racket is tilted to the left to create a half sidespin motion (Figure 7-7). The right slice drop shot is different. The racket motion starts behind the head toward the left-front to brush the left-back part of the shuttlecock (Figure 7-8). The flights of these slice drop shots are shown in Figure 7-9.

Figure 7-7. Contact of the left slice drop shot

Figure 7-8. Contact of the right slice drop

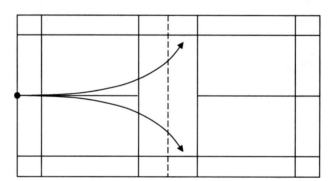

Figure 7-9. Flights of slice drop shots

The backhand overhead drop shot is performed as follows:
- Start with the last step of the backhand footwork.
- The right foot takes the last step with the player's back toward the opponent; swing back toward the left across the body (Figure 7-10).
- Rotate the trunk and the right shoulder back fast, with the elbow leading the racket to swing lightly at the bird; contact the bird at the back of the shoulder with the wrist snapping (Figure 7-11).

Figure 7-10. Rotate and swing back

Figure 7-11. Contact and follow through

Returning overhead drop shots (Figure 7-12):

- Net drop shot if opponents are slow or stay back (#1).
- Push shot to the back corners (#2) if opponents move toward the net.
- Clear shot back if opponents are moving toward the net (#3).
- Rush (smash) if the shot is high.
- Fake clear shot but use drop shot or fake drop shot but use clear shot.

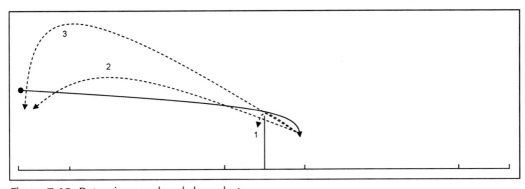

Figure 7-12. Returning overhead drop shots

Tactics:

- Keep the drop shot low and short and close to the net.
- Make motion identical to that of clear and smash shots and combine with clear and smash shots.
- Change speed, spin, and angles.

Training for the Overhead Drop Shot

The training drills for the overhead drop shot are based on game situations. These drills will help players master skills, improve consistency and placement, and work on applications.

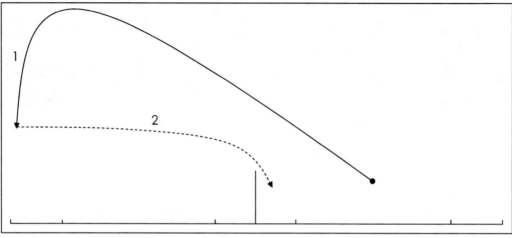

Figure 7-13. Side view of the clear-drop drill

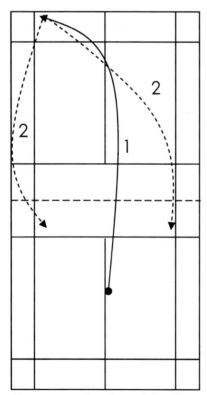

Figure 7-14. Top view of the clear-drop drill

- Clear-drop drill:
  - ✓ The partner feeds with a clear serve, and the player uses forehand, around-the-head, and backhand clear shots to one corner for consistency and placement (Figures 7-13 and 7-14).
  - ✓ The player hits to two corners to work on changing lines.
  - ✓ The partner feeds to two backcourt corners, and the player returns with forehand, around-the-head, or backhand drop shots to work on judgment, movement, and use of proper shots.

- Several combination drills are designed to mix overhead drop shots with other skills similar to game situations. The "clear-clear-clear-drop-clear-smash-drop" drill introduced in Chapter 6 is also a good drill for overhead drop shots. The "clear-drop-drop-drop" drill (Figures 7-15 and 7-16) is a common drill to connect overhead drop shots with net drop shots through footwork. "Clear-drop-drop," "clear-clear-drop-drop," and "clear-clear-clear-drop-drop" drills all work on overhead drop shots in the format of game situations.

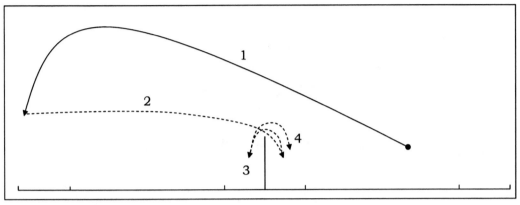

Figure 7-15. Side view of the "clear-drop-drop-drop" drill

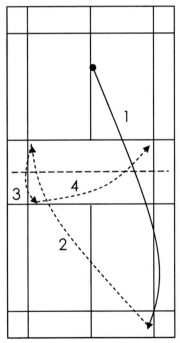

Figure 7-16. Top view of the "clear-drop-drop-drop" drill

8

Smash

The third major overhead shot in badminton is the smash. The smash is mainly used to hit any high but relatively short shots downward with full power, making it difficult or impossible for opponents to return. If a smash is returned, generally the shot is weak. Therefore, the smash is also called the "winning shot" or "scoring shot." Performing a smash is almost the same as performing an overhead drop shot except that players hit smashes with full power while they hit drop shots lightly.

Smashes can be classified as forehand, around-the-head, and backhand smashes. The forehand smash is used the most since it is strongest shot on the forehand side. The around-the-head smash is used to hit shots on the backhand side within the reachable hitting zone with the forehand grip and motion. The backhand smash is used to hit short shots on the backhand side with the backhand grip. The around-the-head smash and the backhand smash return shots on the backhand side, and both shots are used only in midcourt and frontcourt attacks. The forehand smash is used anywhere from the backcourt to the frontcourt.

Smashes include the flat smash and the slice smash. The flat smash is the basic smash, and it has more power and control. The racket face in a flat smash hits the bird flat downward. The left slice smash changes the flight toward the opponent's right sideline, making it difficult to return. The flat smash and the slice smash use the same motion except that the racket is tilted toward the left at contact in a slice smash.

Skills and Applications

Purposes:
- Finish the rally.
- Force mistakes or weak returns.

Applications:
- The shuttlecock is above the net and in the smash zone.
- To opponents who are weak at returning the smash.
- Forehand smash at the back through the frontcourt; around-the-head and backhand smashes at the frontcourt or midcourt.

Pathway (Figure 8-1): The smash comes straight downward toward the opponent's chest or the sidelines.

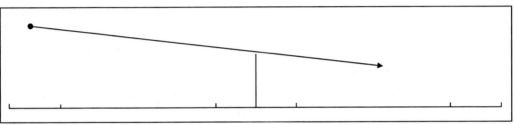

Figure 8-1. Smash pathway

Performance:

The forehand smash is performed as follows:
- Start with the basic stance; move into position and be ready (Figure 8-2).
- Shift body weight toward the right foot, jump, and swing back (Figure 8-3).
- Rotate the body to the left, full swing forward, and hit the bird at the far up-front of the right shoulder with the wrist snapping (Figure 8-4).
- Land with the left foot first at the back and then the right foot; follow through with the racket to the left (Figure 8-5).

The around-the-head smash is performed as follows:
- Move and face the opponent; turn the right shoulder back slightly, and swing back (Figure 8-6).
- The racket swings overhead; hit the shuttlecock, and then follow through to the right (Figure 8-7).

Figure 8-2. Move into position and get ready

Figure 8-3. Jump and swing back

Figure 8-4. Rotate the shoulder and contact

Figure 8-5. Follow through

Figure 8-6. Move and swing back

Figure 8-7. Contact

The backhand smash is performed as follows:

- Move into position, turn back toward the opponent, take right step, and swing back with the shuttlecock behind the up-right shoulder (Figure 8-8).
- Rotate the trunk to start, with the elbow leading and the wrist snapping downward (Figure 8-9).

Figure 8-8. Move and swing back

Figure 8-9. Contact

Returning smashes (Figure 8-10):

- Slice drop back or block back if opponents are away from the net (#1).
- Drive back if the smash is high (#2).
- Clear back if the shot is low and opponents move forward (#3).

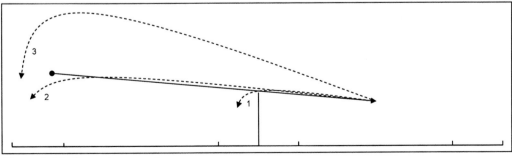

Figure 8-10. Returning smashes

Returning smashes with drive or clear shots places the shuttlecock into the opponent's backcourt so that his next move is not aggressive. This kind of return is used when the opponent is not strong at the backcourt so that he will not smash again or, if he does, the shot will not be strong. It is also used when the opponent is moving forward to control the net after he smashes.

• Forehand return (Figures 8-11 through 8-14)

Figure 8-11. Rally stance

Figure 8-12. Small swing back

Figure 8-13. Contact the shuttlecock flat forward or upward

Figure 8-14. Follow through

• Backhand return (Figures 8-15 through 8-18)

Figure 8-15. Rally stance

Figure 8-16. Swing back

Figure 8-17. Contact with wrist snap

Figure 8-18. Follow through

- Return with a block: This kind of return uses a block motion to block the shuttlecock to the front corner so that opponents have no time to move forward to catch it or have no chance to hit a smash again. It is used when the opponent is slow at coming back to the center position.
- Forehand return (Figures 8-19 through 8-22)

Figure 8-19. Rally stance

Figure 8-20. Small swing back

Figure 8-21. Contact with a slice or flat smash for a block

Figure 8-22. Follow through

- Backhand return (Figures 8-23 through 8-26)

Figure 8-23. Rally stance

Figure 8-24. Swing back

Figure 8-25. Contact with a slice or flat smash for a block

Figure 8-26. Follow through

Tactics:
- Smash
  - ✓Smash to the openings, the two sidelines, the two backcourt corners, and the opponent's chest.
  - ✓Make the smash motion identical to that of overhead clear and overhead drop shots, and alternate the three shots to confuse opponents.
- Return
  - ✓Return to the openings, and change angles.
  - ✓Make drive, clear, and drop shot motions identical, and alternate these three returns.

Training for the Overhead Smash

The drills for the overhead smash are based on game situations. These drills will help players master skills, improve consistency and placement, and work on applications.

- Clear-smash drill:
    - ✓The partner feeds with a clear serve, and the player hits forehand, around-the-head, and backhand smashes to one target or line for consistency and placement (Figures 8-27 and 8-28).
    - ✓The player hits to two lines to work on changing lines.
    - ✓The partner feeds to two backcourt corners, and the player work on judgment, movement, and hitting lines. For around-the-head and backhand smashes, the partner should feed with shorter clears.

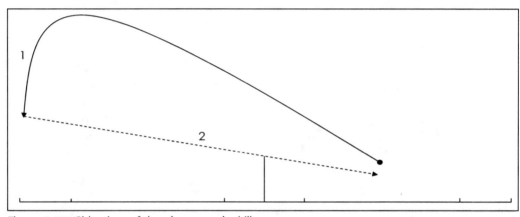

Figure 8-27. Side view of the clear-smash drill

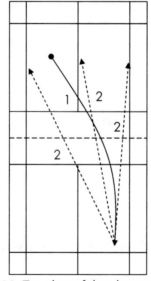

Figure 8-28. Top view of the clear-smash drill

- Clear-smash-drop drill (Figures 8-29 and 8-30): Players can work on underhand clear shots, returning smashes with drop shots and blocks, and footwork. Players should start with easy smashes and then proceed to harder smashes later. Changing smash targets and returning angles can be added later to make the drill more like a game situation.

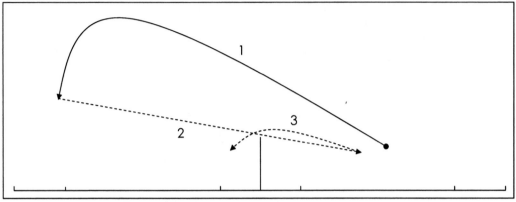

Figure 8-29. Side view of the clear-smash-drop drill

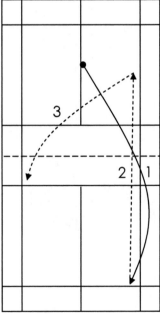

Figure 8-30. Top view of the clear-smash-drop drill

- Clear-smash-clear-smash-drop drill (Figures 8-31 and 8-32): Players mainly work on returning smashes with clear and drop shots alternately to confuse opponents. They also work on smashes and footwork.

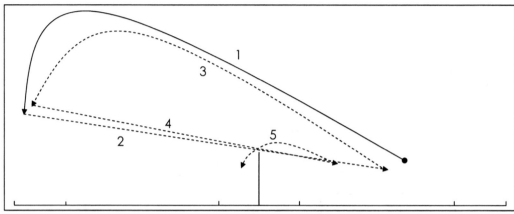

Figure 8-31. Side view of the clear-smash-clear-smash-drop drill

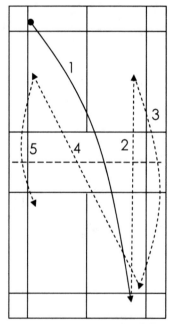

Figure 8-32. Top view of the clear-smash-clear-smash-drop drill

- Clear-smash-clear-drop-drop drill (Figures 8-33 and 8-34): Players combine an underhand clear shot, a smash, an underhand clear shot, an overhead drop shot, and a net drop shot. They work on combining smash and overhead drop shot skills together with identical motions to confuse opponents.

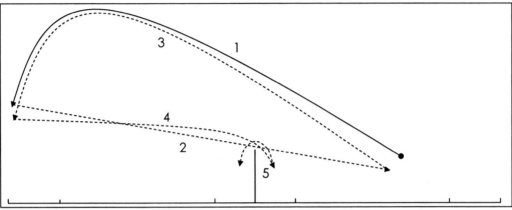

Figure 8-33. Side view of the clear-smash-clear-drop-drop drill

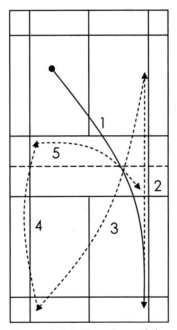

Figure 8-34. Top view of the clear-smash-clear-drop-drop drill

- Clear-drop-clear-smash-drop drill (Figures 8-35 and 8-36): This drill is similar to the clear-smash-clear-drop-drop drill except that the order of the smash and the overhead drop shot is switched. This drill will provide players with flexible hitting options for the smash and drop.

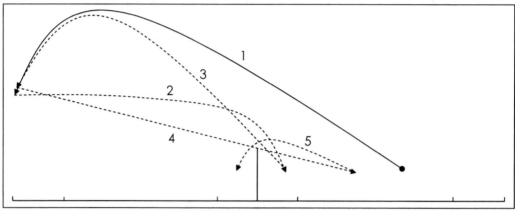

Figure 8-35. Side view of the clear-drop-clear-smash-drop drill

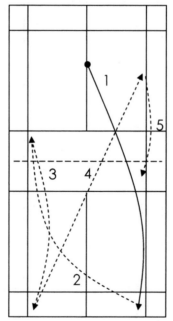

Figure 8-36. Top view of the clear-drop-clear-smash-drop drill

9

Drive Shot and Push Shot

DRIVE SHOT

Skills and Applications

Drive shots are fast shots like smashes except that in drive shots the shuttlecock travels forward while in smashes the bird travels downward. Drive shots are mainly performed at the midcourt and frontcourt to return flat shots above the waist level. Drive shots are usually used in doubles games since players can hit fast and still keep the shot low to avoid smashes.

Drive shots are categorized as forehand, around-the-head, and backhand shots. The forehand drive is used to return shots on the forehand side. The around-the-head drive is used to hit shots on the backhand side when the bird is above the shoulder level with the forehand grip. The backhand drive is used to hit shots on the backhand side with the backhand grip, especially when the shot is too low to make with the around-the-head shot.

Drive shots have flat and slice forms. The flat drive shot is the basic shot when the shuttlecock is hit in the flat forward form. The flat drive shot has more power and can go far and fast. The slice drive shot is done with a backspin motion, and then the shuttlecock drops short instead of flying long and deep, which can confuse opponents.

Purposes:
- Keep the bird flat and fast to avoid smashes.
- Catch an opening before opponents cover it.
- Use speed to force mistakes or weak returns.

Applications:
- When opponents are strong at smashes.
- When opponents have openings.
- When opponents are slow.
- Used more in doubles games.

Pathway (Figure 9-1): The drive shot flies parallel to the floor, aiming at the opponent's chest or openings and backcourt corners for flat drive shots (#1) and aiming short in the midcourt for slice drive shots (#2).

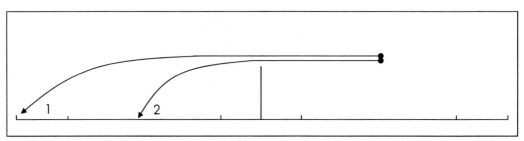

Figure 9-1. Flat drive and slice drive shots

Performance:

The forehand flat drive shot is performed as follows:
- Start from the rally stance (Figure 9-2).
- Move to position while swinging back (Figure 9-3).
- Hit the bird with a flat motion toward the target (Figure 9-4).
- Follow through forward to the left (Figure 9-5).

Figure 9-2. Rally stance

Figure 9-3. Move to position and swing back

Figure 9-4. Contact the bird with a flat motion

Figure 9-5. Follow through

The forehand slice drive shot is performed as follows:
- Start from the rally stance (Figure 9-6).
- Move to position while swinging back (Figure 9-7).
- Contact the bird with a backspin motion to hit short (Figure 9-8).
- Follow through forward (Figure 9-9).

Figure 9-6. Rally stance

Figure 9-7. Step and swing back

Figure 9-8. Contact with a slice shot

Figure 9-9. Follow through

The around-the-head drive shot is performed as follows:
- Start from the rally stance (Figure 9-10).
- Move for good positioning while swinging back around the head with the hand above the head and the racket behind the left shoulder (Figure 9-11).
- Hit the bird with a flat motion toward the target (Figure 9-12).
- Follow through forward to the right (Figure 9-13).

Figure 9-10. Rally stance

Figure 9-11. Swing back to the left

Figure 9-12. Contact

Figure 9-13. Follow through to the right

The backhand flat drive shot is performed as follows:
- Start from the basic stance (Figure 9-14).
- Position and swing back with the back toward the opponent (Figure 9-15).
- Hit the bird with a flat motion toward the target (Figure 9-16).
- Follow through forward to the right (Figure 9-17).

Figure 9-14. Rally stance

Figure 9-15. Position and swing back

Figure 9-16. Contact

Figure 9-17. Follow through

The backhand slice drive shot (Figure 9-18) is performed the same as the backhand flat drive shot except that the racket is tilted and the follow-up motion is small.

Figure 9-18. Slice drive shot at contact

Returning drive shots (Figure 9-19):
- Drop or block if opponents settle in the midcourt or backcourt (#1).
- Drive back in most cases (#2).
- Clear back if opponents are moving forward (#3).

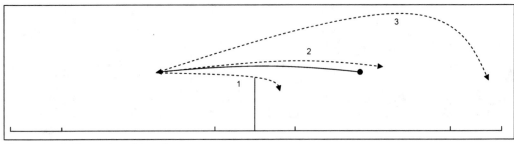

Figure 9-19. Returning drive shots

Tactics:
- Target at openings or dead spots.
- Make the flat drive shot and slice drive shot motions identical and alternate both shots.
- Chance angles.
- Combine with other slice, drop, and clear shots.

Training for the Drive Shot

The training drills for the drive shot are based on game situations. These drills will help players master skills, improve consistency and placement, and work on applications.
- The basic drive shot rally is performed as follows (Figure 9-20):
    - ✓Players rally forehand-to-forehand and backhand-to-backhand for consistency and crosscourt placement.
    - ✓Players rally forehand-to-backhand for down-the-line placement.
    - ✓For practice of drive shots in doubles games, the player moves forward for an offensive drive shot, while the partner moves backward for a defensive drive shot.

Figure 9-20. Side view of the drive shot rally drill

- The four-lines drive shot rally (Figure 9-21) is performed as follows:
  - ✓ The player hits a down-the-line drive shot, and the partner hits crosscourt shots.
  - ✓ Both players hit two lines randomly.

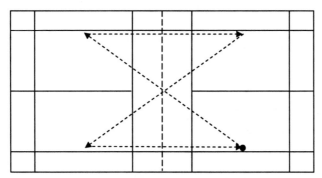

Figure 9-21. Top view of the drive shot rally drill

PUSH SHOT

Skills and Applications

The push shot is similar to the drive shot in terms of the pathway and hitting motion except that it does not have a big backswing motion like the drive shot. The push shot mainly uses forearm and wrist motions to place the shuttlecock toward the targets: backcourt corners, midcourt sidelines, or the opponent's chest. The push shot is a frontcourt skill, and it works best with the net drop shot to confuse opponents.

Purposes:
- Hit the bird flat and fast to targets.
- Catch an opening before an opponent covers it.

Applications:
- To opponents who are moving forward.
- To opponents who have openings at the backcourt corners and midcourt sidelines.
- To opponents who are slow.
- Alternate with net drop shots.

Pathway (Figure 9-22): The push shot flies parallel to the floor, aiming at the opponent's chest, the backcourt corners (#1), or the sidelines (#2).

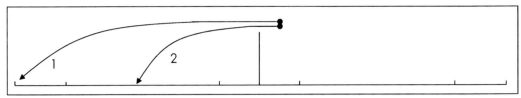

Figure 9-22. Pathway of the push shot

Performance:

The forehand push shot is performed as follows:

- Take a right step forward and hold the racket high at the net level, (Figure 9-23) with the forehand grip.
- Before contact, rotate the forearm and wrist to keep the racket facing forward, and then use forearm and wrist power to hit the shuttlecock flat forward (Figure 9-24).
- Follow through forward (Figure 9-25).

Figure 9-23. Move and prepare

Figure 9-24. Hit the bird flat forward

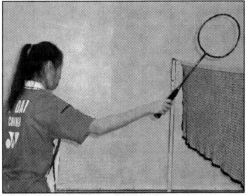
Figure 9-25. Follow through

The backhand push shot is performed as follows:
- Take a right step forward and hold the racket high at the net level, with a backhand grip (Figure 9-26).
- Before contact, rotate the forearm and wrist to keep the racket facing forward, and then use forearm and wrist power to hit the shuttlecock flat forward (Figure 9-27).
- Follow through forward (Figure 9-28).

Figure 9-26. Step and prepare

Figure 9-27. Hit the bird flat forward

Figure 9-28. Follow through

Returning push shots:
- Block if the bird is coming toward the body.
- Drive or drop shot back if the player can get into position.

Tactics:
- Catch the birdie early (high and close to the net).
- Make the push shot and net drop motions identical and alternate both shots to confuse the opponent.
- Push shots to different lines and targets.

Training for the Push Shot

The training drills for the push shot are based on game situations. These drills will help players master skills, improve consistency and placement, and work on applications.

- Feed and push shot drill:
    - ✓ The partner feeds to the player's forehand and backhand, and the player makes push shots accordingly to one line.
    - ✓ The partner feeds to the player, and the player makes push shots to two lines alternately.
    - ✓ The partner feeds to two spots alternately, and the player moves using forehand and backhand push shots accordingly.
- Serve and push shot drill: The partner makes short serves to different corners, and the player returns with push shots accordingly.
- Alternate with net drop shots drill: The partner feeds to the player's forehand or backhand, and the player alternates down-the-line and crosscourt push shots and down-the-line and crosscourt net drop shots.

10

Net Drop Shot

Net drop shots are used in the frontcourt to keep shots low and close to the net. Net drop shots can be classified as forehand and backhand shots, down-the-line and crosscourt shots, and slice drop and lift drop shots. A spin motion is mainly used in net drop shots to keep the shuttlecock flipping, staying low and close to the net. The forehand net drop shot uses a forehand grip, and the backhand net drop shot uses a backhand grip.

Skills and Applications

Purposes:
- Make the shuttlecock drop close to the net to win the rally.
- Force weak returns or mistakes.
- Make opponents lift up and then attack.
- Keep the shuttlecock low to make opponents less aggressive.

Applications:
- To opponents who are in the backcourt or step back.
- To opponents who are weak at net play.
- Combine with clear and push shots.

Pathway: The net drop shot flies in a half circle, targeting the frontcourt corners (Figure 10-1), and can be hit both down-the-line (Figure 10-2) and crosscourt (Figure 10-3).

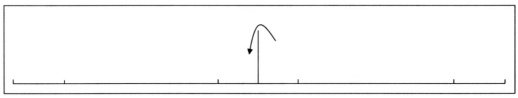

Figure 10-1. Side view of net drop shot pathways

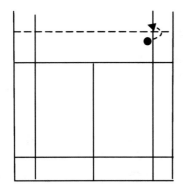

Figure 10-2. Down-the-line net drop shot

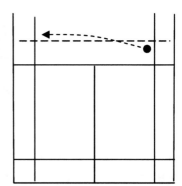

Figure 10-3. Crosscourt net drop shot

Performance:

The flight pattern of the slice net drop shot is demonstrated in Figure 10-4. The back slice motion with a forehand or backhand grip makes the shuttlecock flip backward and remain low.

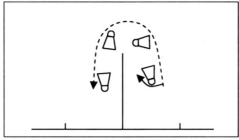

Figure 10-4. Bird flip motion of a slice net drop shot

The forehand down-the-line slice net drop shot is performed as follows:
- Right step with the racket vertical at the net level and parallel to the net (Figure 10-5).
- The wrist snaps so that the racket slices the bird down and forward (Figure 10-6).
- The racket follows through forward (Figure 10-7).

Figure 10-5. Step and prepare

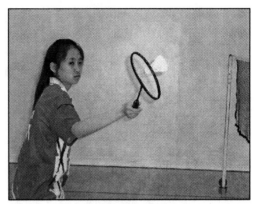
Figure 10-6. Slice the shuttlecock

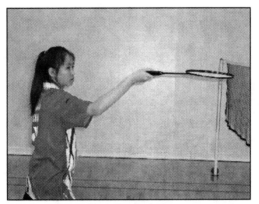
Figure 10-7. Follow through

The backhand down-the-line slice net drop shot is performed as follows:

- Right step with the racket vertical at the net level and parallel to the net (Figure 10-8).
- The wrist snaps so that the racket slices the bird down and forward (Figure 10-9).
- The racket follows through forward (Figure 10-10).

Figure 10-8. Step and prepare

Figure 10-9. Slice the shuttlecock

Figure 10-10. Follow through

The forehand crosscourt slice net drop shot is performed as follows:

- The right foot steps into position with the racket vertical at the net level (Figure 10-11).
- Slice the bottom of the bird down and then toward the left (Figure 10-12).
- The racket follows through to the left (Figure 10-13).

Figure 10-11. Step and prepare

Figure 10-12. Slice the shuttlecock to the left

Figure 10-13. Follow through

The backhand crosscourt slice net drop shot is performed as follows:
- Right step into position with the racket vertical at the net level (Figure 10-14).
- Slice the bottom of the bird down and then forward toward the right (Figure 10-15).
- The racket follows through to the right (Figure 10-16).

Figure 10-14. Step and prepare

Figure 10-15. Slice the shuttlecock to the right

Figure 10-16. Follow through

The lift net drop shot is like the slice net drop shot except that it is used to return shots that are very close to the net, thus making it difficult to use slice net drop shots because the racket may hit the net easily. The motion is the reverse motion of the slice net drop shot, and then the shuttlecock flips forward and remains low (Figure 10-17).

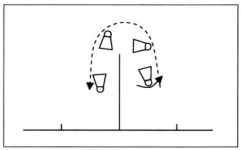

Figure 10-17. Shuttlecock flip motion in the lift net drop shot

The forehand lift net drop shot is performed as follows:

- Right step with the racket flat at the net level and close to the net (Figure 10-18).
- When the bird is falling down toward the racket, slide the racket to the right along the net at the same time with the wrist snapping back and then up so that the racket lifts the bird upward (Figure 10-19).
- The racket follows through up forward (Figure 10-20).

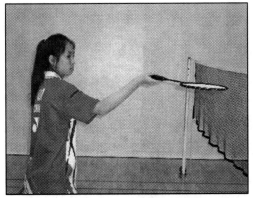

Figure 10-18. Step and prepare

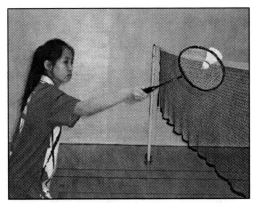

Figure 10-19. Topspin motion

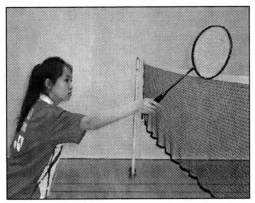

Figure 10-20. Follow through

The backhand down-the-line lift slice net drop shot is performed as follows:

- Right step with the racket flat at the net level and close to the net (Figure 10-21).
- When the bird is falling toward the racket, slide the racket to the left along the net at the same time with the wrist snapping back and then up so that the racket lifts the bird backward and then upward with a topspin motion (Figure 10-22).
- The racket follows through up forward (Figure 10-23).

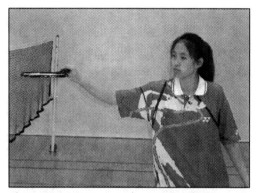
Figure 10-21. Step and prepare

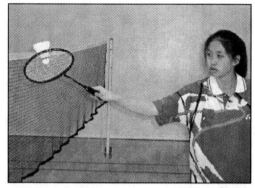
Figure 10-22. Topspin motion to lift the bird

Figure 10-23. Follow through

Returning net drop shots (Figure 10-24):

- Net drop back if opponents move back, or use crosscourt net drop shot if it is too close to the net (#1).
- Rush if the shot is high (#2).
- Push shot to back corners if the shot is at the net level (#3).
- Underhand clear shot back if the shot is too low (#4).

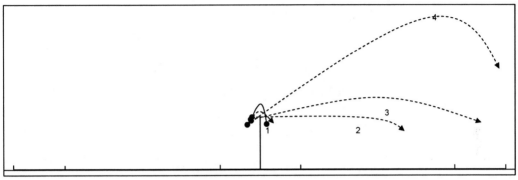

Figure 10-24. Returning net drop shots

Tactics:

- Reach high at the top level of the net (do not let the bird drop low).
- Slice (chop) so that the shuttlecock will flip and remain low, and keep the shuttlecock as close to the net as possible.
- Confuse opponents by combining down-the-line and crosscourt net drop shots and by combining net drop shots with push and clear shots.

Training for the Net Drop Shot

The training drills for the net drop shot are based on game situations. These drills will help players master skills, improve consistency and placement, and work on applications.

- Feed and net drop shot drill:

   ✓The partner feeds to the player's forehand and backhand, and the player makes down-the-line and crosscourt net drop shots.

   ✓The partner feeds the player, and the player makes down-the-line and crosscourt net drop shots alternately.

   ✓The partner feeds to the player's forehand and backhand alternately, and the player moves to use forehand and backhand net drop shots accordingly down-the-line or crosscourt.

- Serve and net drop shot drill: The partner makes short serves to different corners, and the player returns with drop shots accordingly.

- Alternate with push shots drill: The partner feeds to the player's forehand or backhand, and the player alternates down-the-line and crosscourt net drop shots and down-the-line and crosscourt net push shots.
- Net drop shot rally drill (Figures 10-25 and 10-26): The player practices down-the-line net drop shot and crosscourt net drop shot rallies with the partner, using a certain pattern first and then trying random rallies.

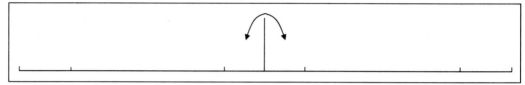

Figure 10-25. Side view of the net drop shot rally drill

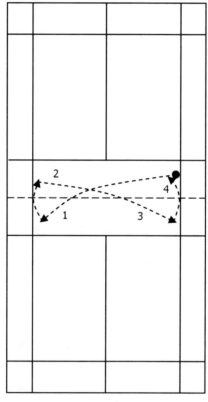

Figure 10-26. Top view of the net drop shot rally drill

11

Singles Game Strategies

This chapter introduces basic singles game strategies for badminton. Included are general strategies, serving strategies, receiving strategies, rally strategies, strategies for single players with different styles, tournament strategies for all players, and training for singles games.

General Strategies

General strategies are commonly used in singles games. The application of these strategies varies with individual players. Based on these general strategies, individual players will also further apply their specific strategies in games.

- Have confidence in your skill and ability.
- Have a good warm-up and enough practice before starting the game.
- Control the rhythm of the game and force opponents to follow your pace.
- React fast to opponents' strategies and styles, and make adjustment immediately.
- Use your best skills and strategies; stick with successful strategies and skills when they work effectively.
- Adjust skills and strategies if they do not work effectively, or when opponents get used to your styles and strategies.
- Save your energy, and wear out opponents by forcing them to move to all corners.
- Find and avoid opponents' strengths, and attack their weaknesses; at the same time, try to use your own strengths, and hide your weaknesses.

Serving Strategies

- Figure 11-1 illustrates all serving options for singles games. Players can alternately use short serves (#1), drive serves (#2), offensive clear serves (#3), and defensive clear serves (#4), and as well as combinations.

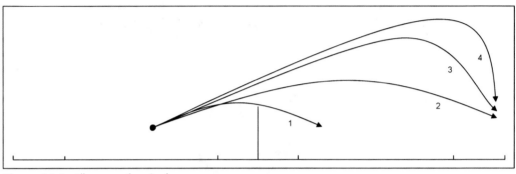

Figure 11-1. All serves for singles games

- Use your best serves at the beginning; if this strategy works, stick with it. When it does not work or opponents get used to it, change to your next good serve.
- Serve long to the backhand corner to see how opponents react, and then adjust to it.
- Alternate offensive clear and defensive clear serves, and observe which one opponents do not return well.
- Use several short serves to the front corners to see how well opponents return them, and then make adjustments.
- Use drive serves several times to test opponents' returning abilities.
- Alternate offensive clear, defensive clear, drive, and short serves to confuse opponents.
- Make all serving motions identical.
- Combine a short serve and a clear serve to the diagonal corners (Figure 11-2).
- Combine a drive serve to the inside corner and a short serve to the outside corner (Figure 11-3).

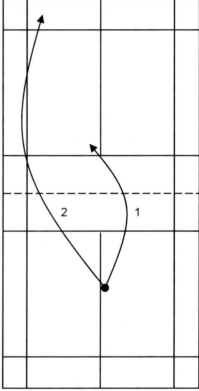

Figure 11-2. Short serve-clear serve combination

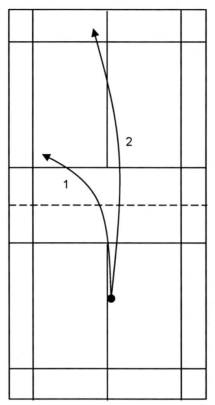

Figure 11-3. Drive serve-short serve combination

- Use backhand clear, drive, and short serves to catch opponents off-guard if you have the skills; these serves are usually fast and low, making it difficult for opponents to return with strong shots.

Receiving Strategies

Returning Clear Serves

- Figure 11-4 demonstrates all three returning shots (#1, drop shot; #2, smash; #3, clear shot). Placements of these returns are shown in Figure 11-5 (#1 and #3, drop shot; #2 and #4, clear shot; #5 and #6, smash).
- Anticipate opponents' serves and move into position immediately.
- Return to the opponent's backhand corner with offensive clear shots once or several times to force weak returns, and then use a slice net drop shot toward the opponent's right-front corner.

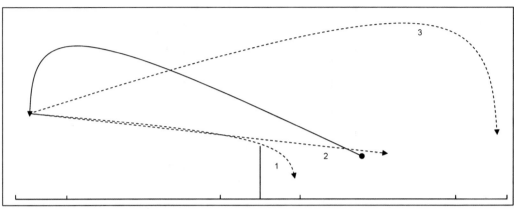

Figure 11-4. Returning clear serves (pathways)

• After a player has returned a serve to the backhand corner at the backcourt, the opponent tends to move back to the backhand corner for subsequent serves, thus creating a good opportunity to return the serve with a quick slice net drop shot to the opening at his right-front corner. Alternately returning serves to the backhand and right-front corners will confuse the opponent, making him hesitate about his movements and shots.

• Hit to the opponent's backhand back corner suddenly after hitting to the forehand corner several times, which causes another opening; this strategy works better with combinations with drop shots to his left-front corner.

• Hit in the opposite direction of the opponent's movement; hit clear back if the opponent is moving toward the net, and hit a net drop shot if the opponent stays back or is moving back.

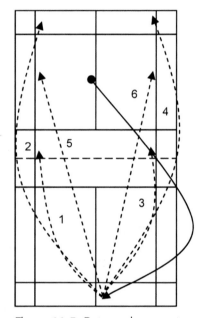

Figure 11-5. Return placements

• Take any opportunities to smash in the midcourt and frontcourt when the opponent serves short or makes a weak return.

• Fake a clear shot with a big motion similar to that of a clear shot but make a net drop shot instead, or fake a net drop shot with a small motion but make a clear shot back to confuse opponents.

Returning Short Serves

- Figure 11-6 illustrates the four ways to return short serves (#1, net drop shot; #2, rush shot; #3, drive shot; #4, clear shot). Placements of these returns are demonstrated in Figure 11-7 (#1 and #2, net drop shot; # 3 and 4, drive shot; #5 and #6, clear shot).
- Anticipate opponent's serve, and move into position immediately.
- Return the short serve with a quick push shot to the back corners if you can catch the bird high; this strategy works effectively if the opponent is slow.
- Return to opponent's backhand corner with underhand clear shots to force weak returns, and then get ready to put it away.
- Hit a drop shot when your opponent is moving back to the backcourt to catch the opening and to make the opponent hesitate if he moves back for a potential long shot or stays for a short return.
- Alternately return to front and back corners to confuse opponents.
- Hit to the opposite direction of opponent's movement; hit a clear shot back if the opponent is moving toward the net, or hit a net drop shot if the opponent stays back or is moving back.
- Fake a clear or push shot with a big motion but hit a drop net shot instead or fake a net drop with a small motion but hit a clear or push shot back with a small motion to confuse opponents; keeping the clear or push and net drop shot motions identical is the key element of this strategy.

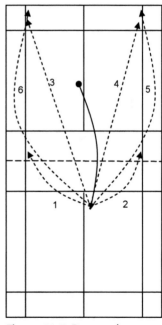

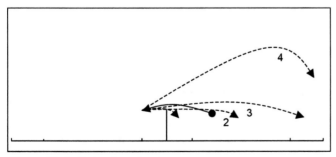

Figure 11-6. Returning short serves   Figure 11-7. Return placements

Returning Drive Serves

- Figure 11-8 demonstrates the two ways to return a drive serve (#1, net drop shot; #2, drive or clear shots). Placements of these two returns are shown in Figure 11-9 (#1 and #3, net drop shot; #2 and #4, drive or clear shot).
- Anticipate opponent's serve, and move into position immediately.
- Return a drive serve with a quick drive shot to the sidelines or the back corners if you can catch the bird in a good position.
- Hit overhead or underhand drop shots when your opponent is moving back to the backcourt or staying in the midcourt.
- Just block back if you are not in a good position.
- Fake a return with a clear shot but hit a net drop shot instead.

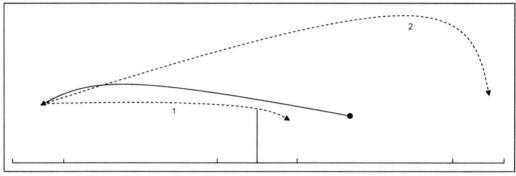

Figure 11-8. Returning drive serves

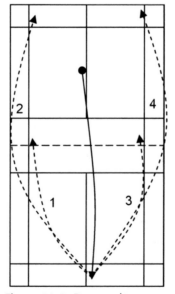

Figure 11-9. Return placements

Rally Strategies

- Attack the backcourt, especially the backhand corner, to force weak returns or mistakes, and then take any opportunities to attack the frontcourt openings.
- Move the opponent to the four corners to wear him out or force weak returns or mistakes, and take any opportunities to attack the openings or smash at any high shots in the frontcourt or midcourt.
- Alternate a fast attack to the backcourt and a fast net drop shot to the frontcourt for net play.
- Hit net drop shots several times, and then hit a push shot back when the opponent is staying in the frontcourt.
- Attack opponent's sides hard to force weak returns or mistakes, and then control the net.
- Play defensively by returning all shots, let opponents make mistakes, and catch openings to attack.
- Fake clear shots but hit net drop shots and fake net drop shots but hit clear shots back using single identical motions.
- Fake smashes but hit net drop shots instead and fake net drop shots but hit smashes to confuse opponents.

Singles Playing Styles

Badminton players have different styles, and different styles have specific strategies besides the common strategies. Following are basic styles and strategies for dealing with players of different styles.

Four-Corners Style

The four-corners style is common and used by most badminton players. Players with the four-corners style usually use clear and net drop shots to move opponents to all four corners in badminton. This style of play results in opponents getting tired and making mistakes or returning with weak shots so that players can smash to win; it also results in opponents who cannot get into positions for proper shots, thus leave more openings.

The following strategies can be used to counter players who use the four-corners style:

- Use the same strategies to deal with these players, especially when you have good endurance; a player with four-corners style only means that he tends to hit shots to the opponent's four corners but does not necessarily deal well with the same strategy when opponents use it.

- Attack opponent's weak spots or open spots so that he will be busy saving his shots instead of placing shots well on your side.
- Figure out opponent's skills, playing patterns, and habits, and then use shots that he cannot return well to ruin his placement.
- Play aggressively to force the opponent to follow your rhythm and game pace, and dominate the game so that he cannot use his style easily.

Aggressive Style

The aggressive style usually includes more smashes to force mistakes or weak returns and to control the net. Players with this style tend to make opponents nervous by making them play under pressure, therefore making more mistakes. They tend to press opponents to follow their style and finish the game in a short time, before opponents figure out a strategy. The men's single champion of the 2008 Olympics uses this style.

The following strategies can be used to counter players who use the aggressive style:
- An aggressive player must have a good setup (e.g., lots of clear shots from an opponent) to smash; hitting more offensive clear, net drop, and drive shots will ruin his opportunities to attack, making him feel that his style is useless against you.
- Play defensively if you have good endurance and defensive skills (such as returning smashes); aggressive style of play gets players tired easily, therefore playing defensively can exhaust opponents in a short time so that you can start your attack.

Defensive Style

The defensive style is based on using outstanding defensive skills to make opponents tired, which makes them make mistakes or hit weak returns. Players with the defensive style tend to slow down the pace of the game and make opponents follow their style, making opponents change their playing patterns to something they are not comfortable or familiar with. Defensive style players also want to wear opponents out.

The following strategies can be used to counter players who use the defensive style:
- Play fast to change the opponent's playing patterns so that he cannot use his favorite skills and patterns, making him feel that his style is useless against you.
- Play aggressively, especially if you are a strong and aggressive player.

Finesse Touch Style

The finesse touch style includes more controlled shots to place the bird at intended targets, especially open spots in games. Players with the finesse touch style usually do not use strong clear shots or smashes; instead, they hit outstanding finesse shots to the openings and weak spots to score, making opponents tired and forcing more weak shots and mistakes. They use more net plays to reduce potential attacks from opponents. These players also try to make opponents give up and change their comfortable playing patterns (such as aggressive plays) to something they are not comfortable or familiar with.

The following strategies can be used to counter players who use the finesse touch style:

- Play fast and aggressively to give the opponent no time to use his finesse skills, forcing him to change his playing patterns and habits so that he cannot use his favorite skills and patterns.
- Move the opponent back and forth to all four corners to tire him out so that he is not performing well, and then attack with aggressive shots.

Tournament Strategies

Tournament strategies, including pre-tournament preparation and during-tournament strategies, prepare players for tournaments and teach players how to adjust in games.

- Find out all the details about the tournament, such as location and gym conditions, date(s) of the tournament, how it is organized, and participants, and then prepare attire, rackets and birds, water, rides, and anything necessary for your team or players.
- Study major opponents' playing habits and styles, strengths and weaknesses of skills, and strategies by watching their previous games and videotapes; talk to people who have played them before. Then train accordingly, making game plans for your team against these players. Besides the main plans, the coach should also prepare alternative plans that can be used when situations are not as ideal as you planned or situations change.
- Watch the games of your major opponents and adjust your strategies and plans if their games are before your games. If you play before your major opponents, you may hide your favorite skills if your opponents are watching so that you can surprise them if you are sure you can win the game you are playing. You may also use psychological tactics before you play your major opponents and during the warm-up, such as looking tired or injured to loosen them up, and then catch them off-guard.

Training for Singles Games

Singles games have unique characteristics, and training for singles games should follow the common singles game patterns. However, players are different, and their individual playing styles should be reflected in training. Following are several guidelines for singles player training:

- Establish good body conditioning. Footwork speed is especially important to movement and positioning in singles games. Endurance is also essential to singles games.
- Develop strong major skills, including forehand and backhand clear shots and overhead drop shots; using these skills alternately and taking opportunities to smash are critical to playing well in singles games.
- Develop fast footwork. The six directions of footwork should be worked on as much as possible to play effectively.
- Play and train with stronger players. It is common practice nowadays that female players play and train with male players to help them hit harder, return harder shots, and move faster.
- Use two players against one in training to force faster movement.
- Use psychological (mental) training. Psychological training is important for badminton players to establish mental toughness so that they can deal with any situation and play consistently. Following are ways to train badminton players psychologically:

    ✓ Do more skills training that is similar to game situations.

    ✓ Play and train with different types of players at different gyms and under different weather conditions to increase experience and mental toughness.

    ✓ Add psychological factors to training and games (e.g., making more noise or getting spectators to yell or laugh so that players can learn how to handle spectator pressure).

    ✓ Train players to deal with unfair calls by referees and unsportsmanlike conduct so that they will control their tempers and not be distracted.

Doubles Game Strategies

This chapter introduces basic doubles game strategies. Included are doubles game formats, rotations for different doubles situations, general strategies, serving strategies, receiving strategies, rally strategies, specific doubles strategies, and training guidelines for doubles games.

Doubles Game Formats

A doubles game format means how two partners share and cover the whole court and how to rotate the format based on the game situation. Only two basic formats exist for double games: the side-by-side format and the front-and-back format. The side-by-side format is used when your side lifts the shuttlecock up, thus putting you in a defensive situation; the front-and-back format is used when your side hits the shuttlecock downward.

Side-by-Side (Defensive) Format (Figure 12-1)

Keyword: Lift
Applications:
- After your side makes a clear serve.
- After your side hits a clear shot.
- After your side makes a flick serve.

Position and coverage:
- Each player covers the court by length, either the left side or the right side.

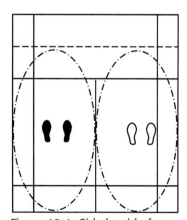

Figure 12-1. Side-by-side format

- Each player covers his own side and moves back and forth.
- Their stance is the rally stance except when receiving the serve.
- Be ready to switch into the front-and-back format when your side hits the shuttlecock downward, such as in smashes or drop shots.

Front-and-Back (Offensive) Format (Figure 12-2)

Keyword: Down

Applications:
- After your side makes a smash.
- After your side makes a drop (overhead or net drop) shot.
- After your side makes a short serve.
- After your side makes a drive shot.
- After your side makes a push shot.
- When your side is serving.

Position and coverage:

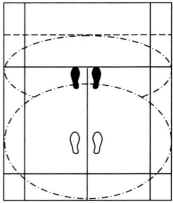

Figure 12-2. Front-and-back format

The center (front) person performs the following:
- Covers the frontcourt (one third of the whole court).
- Moves sideways most of the time.
- Keeps the racket up and is aggressive.
- Uses more rushes, push shots, drop angles, and cutoffs.
- Is ready to move back to the side-by-side format when your side hits the shuttlecock up.

The runner (back) person performs the following:
- Covers the midcourt and backcourt (two thirds of the whole court).
- Moves sideways but to all four corners in his coverage area.
- Be aggressive to the opponent and use fewer upward shots.
- Uses more overhead drop, smash, and drives shots.
- Is ready to move back to the side-by-side format when your side hits the shuttlecock up.

Rotations for Different Doubles Situations

In doubles games, players will not keep the side-by-side format or the front-and-back format at all times. Many rotations and changes will occur based on the game situation. Following are the basic rotation patterns for the doubles format.

Side-by-Side Format to Front-and-Back Format

- When player A makes a net drop shot, he should then move forward to cover the frontcourt, while player B moves back and covers the backcourt (Figure 12-3).
- When player A makes an overhead drop shot or smash from the backcourt, player B should move forward and cover the frontcourt, while player A covers the back (Figure 12-4).

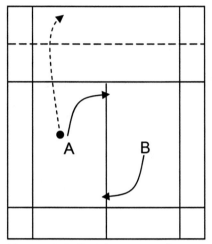

Figure 12-3. Rotation pattern from a net drop shot

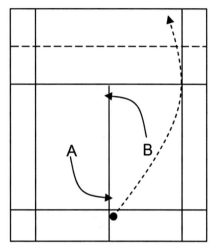

Figure 12-4. Rotation pattern from a smash or overhead drop shot

Front-and-Back Format to Side-by-Side Format

- When player A makes a flick serve, he should then move back to his side (or the other side) to cover that side, while player B should move forward to his side or the opposite side of his partner to cover his side (Figure 12-5).
- When player B makes a clear shot, he should inform his partner to go back, and he moves forward to cover his side; player A should then move back to his side (Figure 12-6).

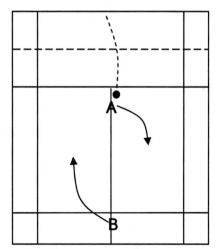

Figure 12-5. Rotation pattern from a flick serve

Two Players' Rotation

Two players on the same side often rotate their positions in the front-and-back format, especially when the runner gets tired from continuous smashing and wants the center person to take over. The runner (player A) must initiate the rotation by hitting a down-the-line smash or drive shot and then keep moving forward to press the opponents by using continuous smashes and drive shots. The partner (player B) needs to rotate back from the other way (Figure 12-7).

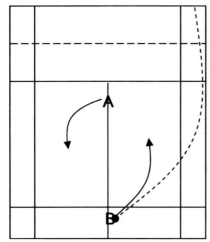

Figure 12-6. Rotation pattern from a clear shot

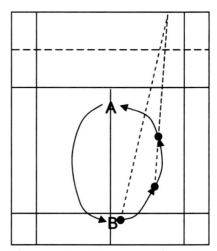

Figure 12-7. Runner and center person rotation

General Doubles Strategies

The application of these strategies varies with players or teams. Based on these general strategies, individual players will further apply their specific strategies in games.

- Prepare teamwork with your partner and communicate well during the game.
- Encourage each other, and never complain about partner's mistakes.
- Have a good warm-up and enough practice before starting the game.
- Control the rhythm of the game, and force opponents to follow your rhythm.
- React fast to opponents' strategies and styles, and make adjustments immediately.
- Know yourself and your partner well, and use both of your strengths; use both of your best skills and strategies. Stick with successful strategies and skills when they work effectively.
- Adjust skills and strategies if they do not work effectively or when opponents get used to your styles and strategies.
- Find out opponents' styles, strengths, and weaknesses of skills and strategies. Avoid opponents' strengths, and attack weaknesses.

Doubles Serving Strategies

- Doubles serves have five targets: the two back corners with flick serves, the two front corners with shorts serves, and the opponent's chest with chasing serves (Figure 12-8).
- Use your best serves to start. If this strategy works well, then stick with it. When it does not work or your opponents get used to it, change to your next good serve.
- Alternate serves to left-front and right-front corners and left-back and right-back corners to test opponents' reactions, and then make necessary adjustments.
- Alternate short and flick serves diagonally to confuse opponents and put pressure on them.
- Serve to one corner several times, and suddenly change to a different corner.
- Look at one corner but serve to another corner to trick opponents.
- Communicate with your partner on what serve you want to use so that he will be prepared.
- Take partner's returning ability into consideration. For example, if your partner cannot return the smash, avoid flick serves; instead use short serves. If your partner is weak at returning low push shots to the backhand corner, then serve to spots where opponents cannot hit push shots (such as with a chasing serve or toward the backhand), or use serves that do not provide opponents such opportunities.
- Make all serving motions identical.

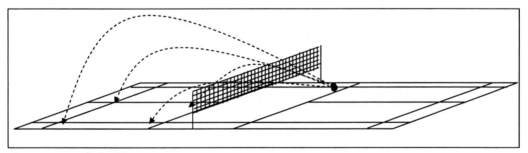

Figure 12-8. All doubles serves

Doubles Receiving Strategies

Returning Flick Serves

- Returns include smashes if you are in good position, drop or block shots if opponents remain in their positions, and clear shots if no chance to attack exists (Figure 12-9).
- Anticipate opponent's serve, and move into position immediately.
- Drop shot to the serving partner's side before he moves up to return.
- Smash if you can move into position.

- Block serve if you are not in a good position or stance to use power or placement.
- Alternately use different returns to confuse opponents.

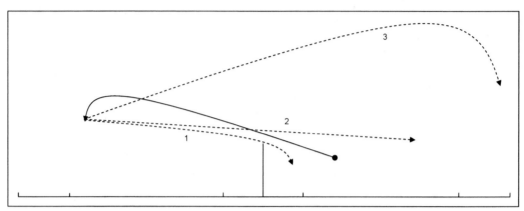

Figure 12-9. Returning flick serves

Returning Short Serves

- Returning short serves involves several techniques. The receiver can use a slice drop shot to the front corners or a drive or push shot to the backcourt corners or lift up to the backcourt if the serve is good. Rushing at the short serve is always the first choice if the serve is high. All returns are based on where the serve is coming: the inside corner (Figures 12-10 and 12-11) or the outside corner (Figures 12-12 and 12-13).
- Anticipate opponent's serve, and move into position immediately.
- Keep returning shots low and close to the net using net drop shots.
- Return to opponent's backhand corner with push shots to force weak returns, and then get ready to put it away.
- Hit between opponents to cause confusion.
- Return to the weaker opponent. If one opponent is strong and the other is weak, your side should try to return shots to the weak opponent as much as possible to force mistakes and weak returns.
- Be aggressive, and rush the serve whenever it is high to put pressure on the server. If the serve is good, try a push or drop shot. Lift up to the backhand corner if no chance to attack exists.
- Hit to the opposite direction of the opponent's movement. Hit a clear shot back if the opponent is moving toward the net, and hit a drop shot if the opponent stays back or is moving back.
- Fake a clear or push shot but hit a drop shot instead, or fake a drop shot but hit a clear or push shot back. Keeping the clear or push and drop shot motions identical is the key element for this strategy.

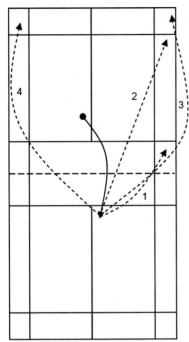

Figure 12-10. Returning an inside-corner serve: right side

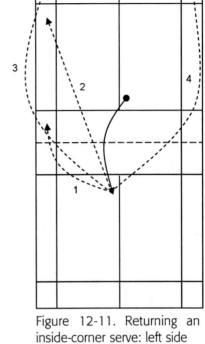

Figure 12-11. Returning an inside-corner serve: left side

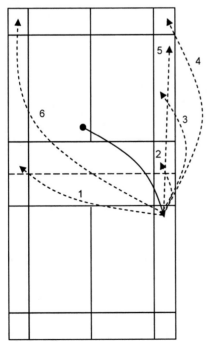

Figure 12-12. Returning an outside-corner serve: right side

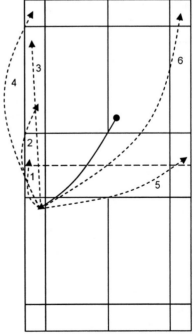

Figure 12-13. Returning an outside-corner serve: left side

Rally Strategies

- Attack the open spots.
- Attack the weak spots such as the backhand corner at the backcourt to force weak returns.
- Attack between opponents (e.g., drop shot or smash to the center when opponents are in the side-by-side format).
- Attack the weak opponent.
- Keep the shots flat if opponents have good smashes.
- Rotate opponents to mess up their format, causing confusion and openings.
- Cover partner's weaknesses.
- Play defensively when opponents are eager to attack aggressively, returning all shots with good placement so that opponents cannot attack easily.

Specific Doubles Strategies

Men's Doubles

Men's doubles games are usually very aggressive. Players tend to use more smashes and fast drive shots whenever they have a chance. Therefore, men's doubles players need to have strong attacking abilities and strong defensive abilities to return smashes. Good placement to open spots is also another characteristic of men's doubles, especially at world top-level competitions. In the Unites States, "A" and "B" level players usually have better placement besides powerful smashes, and they have clear formats and rotations. At the "C" level, smashes are mainly combined with drop shots, but control of placement is lacking, although they have basic teamwork. At the "D" level, players tend to focus more on skills and applications rather than teamwork. At the high school level, varsity players can play at the "C" level; junior varsity players usually have weak skills, and, therefore, their strategies are basic and simple.

Women's Doubles

Women's doubles games are usually less aggressive than men's doubles games. Women players tend to use more clear and drop shots to move opponents and to hit to the openings, and then they take opportunities to smash in the midcourt or frontcourt. In women's doubles, smashes at the backcourt occur less frequently even at world top-level competitions because these smashes are not very strong; therefore, women usually cannot win a rally with long smashes. "A" and "B" level players in the Unites States can place their shots well, and they have clear formats and rotations. "C" level players usually have basic formats for the game, while "D" level players tend to focus on skills rather than teamwork. High school varsity players usually have decent formats, rotations, and teamwork. Junior varsity players usually have only basic formats.

Mixed Doubles

The major difference between mixed doubles and regular doubles games is the format when the man is serving. The woman usually stays in front when the man is serving right behind her; the man backs up immediately after serving to cover the backcourt, and the woman covers the frontcourt. During the rally, the woman plays more in the frontcourt so that she can use her finesse touch skills and the man can use his power advantage in the backcourt. They, however, play in regular formats in most situations. For example, they stay side-by-side after hitting clear shots and stay front-and-back when they are attacking. In the United States, "A" and "B" level players have the same formats as the international level players, but "C" and "D" level players tend to keep the woman in the front all the time, especially at the high school level no matter if they are playing offense or defense. This strategy is not correct because, when the other side is smashing, the girl in the front becomes an easy target and loses the rally easily in most cases. Furthermore, when the other side is smashing, the man behind must cover the whole court, while the woman in the front has a tough time at that position. In mixed doubles games, players tend to attack the woman most times in offense. In defense, the man tries to cover more area for his partner.

Tournament Strategies

Tournament strategies are important in badminton games. Players should know pre-tournament preparation and during-tournament strategies.

- Find out all details about the tournament, such as location and gym conditions, date(s) of tournament, how it is organized, and participants, and then prepare attire, rackets and birds, water, rides, and anything necessary with your partner.
- Find out major opponents' playing habits and styles, strengths and weaknesses of skills, and strategies by watching their previous games and videotapes and talking to people who have played them before. Then train accordingly, making your team plans against the other team or players. Besides the main plans, you and your partner should also prepare alternative plans so that when situations are not as ideal as you planned or change, you have an alternative plan.
- Watch the games of your major opponents and adjust your strategies and plans if their games are before your games. If you play before your major opponents, you may hide your favorite skills so that you can surprise them if you are sure you can win the game you are playing. You may also use some psychological tactics before you play your major opponents and during the warm-up, such as both of you looking tired or injured to loosen them up, and then catch them off-guard.

Training for Doubles Games

Doubles games are similar to singles games in skills but different in applications. Therefore, training for doubles games should follow the common doubles game patterns. However, players are different, and their individual playing styles and teamwork should be reflected in training. Following are several guidelines for doubles player training:

- Develop strong skills, including overhead clear shots, overhead drop shots, smashes to sidelines, drive shots, push shots, net drop shots, and skills each player needs for their teamwork. All skills should be trained in the framework of a doubles game situation (e.g., the drive shot should be practiced with one person moving forward for an offensive drive and one person moving backward for a defensive drive).

- Work more on rotation and court coverage of the two partners. The rotation and coverage should become automatic reactions for different situations. Besides the regular rotation patterns, both players should also have their specific rotation and coverage plans based on their strengths and weaknesses.

- Play and train with stronger players. It is a common practice nowadays that women players play and train with male players to force them to hit harder, return harder shots, and move faster.

- Develop unique playing patterns based on both players' strengths.

- Use psychological (mental) training. Psychological training is important for doubles players to establish mental toughness so that they can deal with any situation and play consistently. Following are ways to train doubles players psychologically:

    ✓ Do more skills training that is similar to game situations.

    ✓ Play and train with different types of players, at different gyms, and under different weather conditions to increase experience and mental toughness.

    ✓ Add psychological factors to training and games (e.g., making more noise or getting spectators to yell so that players can learn how to handle spectator pressure).

    ✓ Train players to deal with unfair calls by referees and unsportsmanlike conduct so that they will control their tempers and not be distracted.

    ✓ Work on patience and forgiveness. Establish good understanding and communication with partners.

13

Coaching High School Badminton

This chapter discusses the qualifications to be a high school badminton coach, the procedures of coaching high school badminton, and the selection of players. Guidelines for training sessions, tournament preparation, and special training are also reviewed.

A Qualified Badminton Coach

Knows How to Play

A badminton coach does not necessarily need to be a professional player, but he should at least be a decent badminton player. He should be able to perform and demonstrate all the basic skills and application of these skills. The hands-on experience will be an advantage when he coaches players and provides feedback to players. A coach who has never played badminton cannot provide real feedback to players. A coach should be a role model for his players, motivating players to work hard; he also should inspire an enthusiastic attitude toward their games and lives. High school players tend to imitate the coach, and a coach who is a good role model can benefit players in more than one way.

Knows How to Coach

A qualified coach should have a good understanding of badminton. He should know all the skills and the teaching and training of each skill as well as all the drills and the application of these drills to improve players' skills; he should train his players with combinations of these skills to mirror game situations. A coach should be able to recognize his players' problems and help them find solutions. He should know his players well and know how to train them for their best play. A good coach needs to arrange training sessions for many athletes who play at different levels.

Requirements and Procedures

A new coach should get familiar with everything relevant to badminton. First, a coach should check the facility, including the maximum courts, the court floors, the lights, and the distance between the court lines and the wall and between courts. He should ask the school to fix problems so that training is effective and players avoid injuries. If the school cannot fix something, the coach needs to make arrangements for a solution, such as mopping the floor if it is too dusty or slippery. The coach also needs to look over the budget to determine what the team needs to provide, such as shuttlecocks, and if fundraising is needed. Transportation of the team is also an important issue. The coach either must request a school bus for transportation to tournaments or must ask parents to volunteer to drive players.

It is the coach's responsibility that the players meet the school requirements for grades to play on the team. The coach also needs to make sure that players have undergone physical examinations and are in good health before the playing deadline.

Selection of Players

A new coach should look over a list of players from the previous year and investigate their effectiveness. Then, he should consult with these players on the first day before the new players arrive and have a good idea which positions they fit in.

The new coach then should screen all the new players. Two steps are used to screen new players. First, the coach can ask all the new players to do a certain skill and move them based on their forms and shots, putting advanced players on one end of all courts and beginners on the other end. Second, the coach should assign each returning player a new player to practice some drills with, usually the drive shot rally, the clear shot rally drill, the clear-drop drill, the clear shot-smash drill, the net drop shot drill, and, sometimes, footwork. The coach then can ask the returning players about the new players' skills. The coach also can ask the new players to play some games with the returning players to see their actual playing abilities. The coach then should have a draft list ranking the new players through his own observations and feedback from the returning players.

Next, the coach should use singles games to test players' actual playing abilities. Half-court singles games to five points are commonly used during the entire screening process. Of course, full-court singles games are better for screening if enough courts and time are available. The coach should place the top-ranked players on the first court, the second-ranked players on the second court, and so forth. The remaining players will be waiting on the last court; after several games, the coach can take the top two players off the court for the varsity team and continue this process until the roster is full. Then, the coach can select the junior varsity team. After selecting both teams, the coach can put the remaining players on the practice team as alternates.

The last step is to arrange singles and doubles positions. The coach should let each player or team play a couple of games to challenge for the positions. The coach will then decide who plays what positions.

Guidelines for Training Sessions

After determination of each position for the team, the coach should arrange training to prepare players for the upcoming tournaments, which might be only two days away or the following week. At the high school level, coaches usually do not have much time for comprehensive training. Therefore, training should be focused on each singles player and each doubles team.

For singles games, players should focus more on footwork, clear serves and shots, overhead drop and net drop shots, and smashes. Several drills are recommended for basic training after the warm-up: the clear shot rally drill, the clear-drop drill, the clear-smash drill, and the clear-drop-drop-drop drill. Then, several combination drills are recommended to apply these skills to mirror game situations: the serve-clear (to the backhand side) drill, the clear-clear-drop-drop drill, the clear-drop-drop drill, and the clear-clear-clear-drop-drop drill. Both players should use identical motions to hit different shots, and both players need to recognize opponents' shots and return according to where opponents are moving. Refer to the instructions for these drills in Chapter 11.

For offense in doubles games, both players need to take turns practicing frontcourt play and backcourt play. Frontcourt play should focus more on rush, push, and net drop shots, while backcourt play should focus more on overhead drop shots and smashes. Both players should also work on offensive and defensive drive shots in the doubles format. For defense in doubles games, both players should focus on returning smashes, overhead drop shots, and clear shots.

Doubles players should work on the short serve-flick serve combination and follow-up with the proper format. They also need to work on returning different serves and follow-up with the proper format. Both players should work on the side-by-side format and front-and-back format combined with practicing skills.

Mixed doubles games present difficulties in high school badminton. It is understandable that coaches always put girls in the front when boys are serving since girls on high school junior varsity teams usually have weak clear shots. However, it is incorrect to put girls in the front all the time, especially during defense. The girl may play in front as much as possible in offense, but both players should be in the side-by-side format in defense. Many varsity mixed doubles teams also put girls in the front all the time even though they have strong clear shots and smashes. As a result, girls become targets and have a hard time when they are in the front when opponents are in offense, and it is extremely difficult for boys to cover the whole court. Coaches should have girls play like professionals and train them to return and hit with smashes, drop shots, and clear shots with effective footwork.

Preparing for Tournaments

Before playing a tournament, the coach and the returning players should share their information regarding the opponents and the results of the last season. If videotapes of games from the last season are available, the team should watch them and analyze the details.

The next step for preparing for a tournament is to arrange positions. The coach should ask each singles player or doubles team to prepare their own playing strategies for one or two potential opponents and train accordingly. The coach can assist each singles player or doubles team in their preparation and training.

The coach should encourage players or their parents to videotape games; the coach and players can review the tapes for feedback. Then, the coach can use the feedback to adjust training to prepare singles players or doubles teams for the next tournament.

Special Training

The actual tournaments start only a couple of weeks into the high school badminton season. Therefore, a coach does not have enough time to improve each player's playing ability. Furthermore, it is impossible for a coach to observe and train every player on a team. The coach should encourage players to seek outside training. Many classes and workshops are offered in private clubs, gyms, and community centers. These opportunities provide additional training for high school players. Many players like to train outside of the high school team so that they can play their best and feel good about themselves.

The coach can also invite alumni of the team who are high-level players to come back and play with the team. Players often enjoy the opportunity to practice and play with better players and to take challenges. The alumni can also help the coach to train more players individually. The alumni can also teach players and coaches new things that they learned from college badminton.

The coach can also invite high-level players, such as retired former professional players and coaches, to demonstrate for the team. These high-level players and coaches are role models on skills and play, and they can motivate teams to train and play better.

Watching videotapes of professional badminton players is another effective way to improve players' skills and games. Often, it only takes several minutes to open a player's mind and learn new and professional techniques. Watching the best players in the world can motivate players for peak performance.

Multiple Birdies Training

Multiple birds training is a very useful training method in badminton. In multiple birds training, the coach holds more than 20 birds in one arm and tosses or hits out the birds continuously to one or two players for single skill training or combination skill practice. At the same time, another player should collect the birds and put them in stacks near the coach while another player hands the stacks to the coach continuously until the practicing player(s) complete the drill. Players rotate between training and collecting birds.

Following is the step-by-step method of multiple birds training:
- Put birds in stacks (Figure 13-1).
- The stack of birds is held in the slightly bent left arm (for a right-handed coach) so that the stack will stay between the arm and the chest (Figure 13-2).
- The thumb and ring finger (together with the little finger) are used to hold the feather part of the lowest bird of the stack. The index and middle fingers are used to hold the bottom of the lowest bird (Figure 13-3).
- When the coach wants to toss the birds to the practicing player, he simply uses the right hand to grab the bottom of the lowest bird and tosses directly out (Figures 13-4 through 13-6). Remember: it is impossible to toss the birds far, therefore, tossing should only be used for frontcourt skill practice, such as net drops, push shots, rush shots at the two front corners, and a combination of down-the-line net drop, crosscourt net drop, and push shot at the left and right corners.
- When the coach wants to hit birds to the player, he should use the index and middle fingers to drag the bottom of the lowest bird downward and release it while hitting out with the racket in his right hand (Figures 13-6 through 13-8). At the same time, the left arm should quickly thrust downward and back in order to send the second-lowest bird to the index and middle fingers. This hitting option can be used to train backcourt skills, middle court skills, frontcourt skills, and full-court combination skills. Examples include a backcourt clear followed by a net drop, a backcourt drop followed with an underhand clear, a smash followed with a net drop, clears and drops to all four corners, a forehand clear followed with a backhand clear, a left net drop followed with a right net drop, training the doubles rotations, etc.

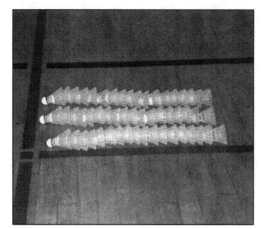

Figure 13-1. Birds in stacks

Figure 13-2. Hold birds between arm and chest

Figure 13-3. Finger position

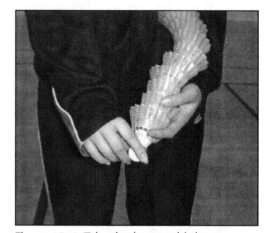

Figure 13-4. Take the bottom bird

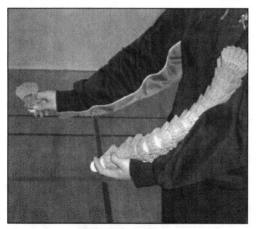

Figure 13-5. Get ready to toss

Figure 13-6. Toss the bird to the target area(s)

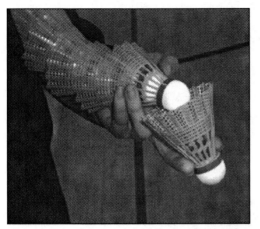

Figure 13-7. Index and middle finger drag the bird down

Figure 13-8. Drop the bird and make a small backswing

Figure 13-9. Hit to the target area(s)

14

Teaching Badminton

This chapter introduces instructional strategies for teaching badminton at middle and high schools and universities. Included are suggested class contents for each level of play and session plans for effective teaching.

Instructional Strategies

Etiquette

Badminton instructors should teach students to be good people. Students should understand badminton's etiquette and manners before they start learning the skills. Using a poster of basic etiquette points and manners, instructors can remind students about these important details at the beginning of each class. Refer to Chapter 1 for badminton etiquette and manners; instructors can select the information that they need for their classes.

Safety Guidelines

Even though badminton is a relatively safe sport, the possibility exists that students can get injured. The instructor should go through the safety guidelines with students at the beginning of the class and stress these rules for the following classes until students develop safe habits while playing badminton. Following safety guidelines is especially important in middle and high school classes.

Several guidelines are important to make badminton safe. A good warm-up always should be done first. A good warm-up should include stretching muscles and rotating all joints, easy running or footwork, and easy rallying. Training students to be aware of what is going on around them and to stay clear of people who are playing can avoid many accidents. Students should be taught to hold onto their rackets when they are hitting because a loose racket may cause injuries to their partners or opponents. In addition, the front player in doubles should never look back when the shuttlecock passes him since the birdie may injure his eye. Students should tell the instructor whenever they feel that a safety problem or risk exists.

Make Learning Fun

Learning and playing badminton should be fun, but it can be boring if practices and games are not properly arranged. Many strategies can be used to make badminton interesting and exciting, especially in beginning classes. It is important that instructors encourage students often instead of pointing out their mistakes. Proper learning takes time, and students need enough practice to develop their skills over time. Students' playing abilities will be much better after 10 to 15 classes, and instructors should be patient to ensure that students are self-confident. From just one critique, students can easily lose their self-esteem and their interest in badminton. The instructor should be careful not to use negative language. Criticism should be left for advanced players and players who have good skills and self-confidence. Instructors should make their students feel successful in badminton.

Counting the numbers of continuous rallies and shots usually makes students feel that badminton is fun and exciting. They consider this kind of performance as an achievement that they can see immediately, especially in front of instructors and partners. Students feel good about themselves, and they will probably continue to play better.

Using little tricks can also make badminton more fun. A common trick is to ask students to pick up shuttlecocks with their rackets. Students can learn this skill in a couple of minutes, and they feel great since advanced players usually do it. Another trick is to use a radar gun to measure the speed of their smashes, which really motivates students to use more body rotation and to play better. The instructor can also play with students or let students challenge him, with other students cheering them on.

Arranging tournaments that imitate world-level games is extremely motivating for students in classes of all levels. Students never tire of this strategy, and enough tournament types exist to maintain variety throughout a semester. By being creative, an instructor can make badminton classes fun and exciting.

Contents for Different Levels of Classes

Contents for different levels of classes are suggested based on the analysis of badminton, the proper learning process, and hands-on experience teaching all different levels of play with feedback from the performance of students in these classes. These contents have been effective for the intended classes. New instructors can use these contents as a starting place and make necessary changes based on their students' needs and other conditions, such as the facility, the equipment, and the availability of time. They should creatively select and apply these contents when they have developed their own hands-on experience and a better understanding of the game.

Contents for Middle and High School Classes

Badminton classes at the middle and high school levels are for beginners. Many students are not strong, and the classes may only last for two to three weeks. It is difficult for most students to develop strong skills and playing ability. Instructors should not expect students to hit long and strong shots. Badminton classes should focus on several basic skills and application of these skills in easy singles and doubles games. Following are contents suggested for classes at this level:

- Warm-up
- Basic stances
- Grips and swings
- Shuttlecock-handling exercises
- Basic two-way footwork
- Clear serves
- Clear shots and the serve-clear shot drill
- Overhead drop shots and the clear clear drop drill
- Smashes and the clear smash-block drill
- Drive shots and the drive shot rally drill
- Net drop shots and the toss-drop drill
- Random clear drop combinations
- Short singles games
- Short doubles games

Contents for Beginning University Classes

Beginning badminton classes at the university level are basically for students who do not have much experience. University students are much stronger than middle and high school students, and they can hit much stronger and better shots. University classes last for one semester or quarter; therefore, players can learn and practice more as well as play more games. However, they are still beginners, and instructors should not expect these students to perform advanced skills. These classes should focus on all basic skills and application of these skills in easy singles and doubles games. Following are contents suggested for classes at this level:

- Basic warm-up
- Basic stances
- Grips and swings
- Shuttlecock-handing exercises
- Basic four-way footwork
- Clear serves, returns, and drills
- Clear shots, returns, and drills
- Overhead drop shots, returns, and drills
- Smashes, returns, and drills
- Drive shots, returns, and drills
- Slice net drop shots, returns, and drills
- Singles games
- Doubles games
- Individual skills evaluation and feedback

Contents for Intermediate University Classes

Intermediate badminton classes at the university level are basically for students who have taken a beginning class or played on a high school team. The students from beginning university classes should have learned all beginning skills and basic application of these skills; however, their skills are usually rough, and they need more practice to improve consistency, placement, and applications in games. The students from high school teams may demonstrate playing experience, and some of them have good skills. However, many high school players have not had proper training, and they often have problems with their skills. Classes at the intermediate university level should focus on continuously improving basic skills, correcting mistakes, learning some intermediate skills (such as backhand overhead drop shots, six-way footwork, etc.), and improving effectiveness of playing games. Following are contents suggested for classes at this level:

- Six-way footwork
- Offensive and defensive clear serves
- Offensive and defensive clear shots
- Forehand and backhand drive shots
- Backhand overhead drop shots
- Smashes to sides and chest, and returns with drive, clear, and block shots
- Crosscourt slices and down-the-line net drop shots
- Combinations drills
    - ✓ Clear-drop-drop-drop drill
    - ✓ Clear-clear-drop-drop drill

- ✓ Clear-clear-clear-drop-drop drill
  - ✓ Clear-drop-drop drill
  - ✓ Clear-smash-drop drill
  - ✓ Clear-smash-clear-smash-drop drill
  - ✓ Clear-smash-clear-drop-drop drill
  - ✓ Clear-clear-clear-drop-clear-smash-drop drill
- Singles game tactic drills
- Doubles game serving tactic drills
- Doubles game receiving tactic drills
- Doubles game format drills
- Round-robin singles
- Round-robin doubles

Contents for Advanced University Classes

Advanced badminton classes at the university level are for students who have good skills and playing abilities. Classes at the advanced level should focus on continuously improving overall skills, learning advanced skills (such as backhand clear shots and smashes, slice smashes and drop shots, etc.), performing high-level drills, developing personalized skills and styles, and trying professional training and playing. Following are contents suggested for classes at this level:

- Special footwork training
- Drive and short serves and combinations with clear serves
- Forehand, around-the-head, and backhand offensive and defensive clear shots hitting four lines
- Forehand and backhand drive shots hitting four lines
- Backhand overhead clear shots and smashes
- Drop shot angles and drop shots from forehand and backhand sides
- Slice smashes and slice drop shots
- Lift net drop shots with forehand and backhand, crosscourt, and down-the-line
- Crosscourt combination drills
  - ✓ Clear-drop-drop-drop drill
  - ✓ Clear-clear-drop-drop drill
  - ✓ Clear-clear-clear-drop-drop drill
  - ✓ Clear-drop-drop drill
  - ✓ Clear-smash-drop drill
  - ✓ Clear-smash-clear-smash-drop drill

- ✓ Clear-smash-clear-drop-drop drill
- ✓ Clear-clear-clear-drop-clear-smash-drop drill
- Multiple-bird training with singles court coverage
- Singles style development for each player
- Doubles game serving and receiving tactic drills
  - ✓ Short serves to the inside corner and returns
  - ✓ Short serves to the outside corner and returns
  - ✓ Flick serves to the inside corner and returns
  - ✓ Flick serves to the outside corner and returns
  - ✓ Combination serves and proper returns
- Doubles format and rotation with multiple-bird drills
- Singles and doubles games that focus on needed skills and strategies
- Body conditioning
- Outside tournaments
- Watching professional games
- Coaching high school teams

Suggested Session Plans

The following sessions are suggested based on common ways of playing and learning badminton, especially through teaching, research, and playing experience. The plans have been used for many years at the university level as well as the middle and high school levels; they have been effective at teaching students how to learn badminton fast and to have fun while learning and playing. These sessions can be adjusted based on the special needs and conditions of each class. Sessions can run longer or shorter, and the instructor can spend more or less time on each skill and drill based on students' progress. Middle and high school classes can be shorter, and university classes can spend more time on practice and games.

After students have learned the basic skills, strategies, and rules of badminton, appropriate tournaments should be arranged to provide them opportunities to apply rules and skills as well as basic tactics in actual games. Playing an actual game is the best way to learn badminton, and it is the ultimate goal of learning badminton. A world-level tournament can be imitated to make the sport more fun, such as Olympic singles with an elimination format, world championship doubles with a round-robin format, or Thomas & Uber or Sudirman Cups for team competitions. Students are extremely motivated when they play these tournaments in university classes, from the beginning level through the advanced level. When instructors are creative, classes are more fun and exciting.

Session 1

- Warm-up
- Two-way footwork
- Forehand and backhand grips
- Underhand and overhead swings
- Drive shot rally
- Underhand clear serves

Session 2

- Warm-up
- Two-way footwork
- Shuttlecock-handling exercises
- Drive shot rally
- Clear serve review
- Clear shot with a clear serve

Session 3

- Warm-up with footwork
- Drive shot rally
- Clear shot rally
- Underhand clear shots with feeding
- Overhead drop shot with an underhand clear shot

Session 4

- Warm-up with footwork
- Drive shot rally
- Clear shot rally
- Clear-drop rally
- Smashes with clear serve and/or shot feeding and block returns

Session 5

- Warm-up with footwork
- Drive shot rally
- Clear shot rally
- Clear-drop rally
- Clear shot-smash-block rally
- Backcourt combination drill (one player hits clear shots only while another player hits clear shots, drop shots, and smashes alternatively with identical motions)

Session 6

- Warm-up with footwork
- Drive shot rally
- Clear shot rally
- Clear-drop rally
- Clear-smash-block rally
- Net drop shots with feeding

Session 7

- Warm-up with footwork
- Clear-drop-drop-drop drill
- Clear-clear-drop-drop drill
- Clear-drop-drop drill
- Clear-clear-clear-drop-drop drill

Session 8

- Warm-up with footwork
- Clear-drop combination
- Singles game strategies
- Singles games

Session 9

- Singles tournaments

Session 10

- Short serves
- Flick serves
- Doubles serving and receiving format (side-by-side and front-and-back formats)
- Doubles game tryout

Session 11

- Short serves and returns
- Flick serves and returns
- Serving and receiving tactics
- Doubles rally format
- Doubles rally tactics
- Doubles games

Session 12

- Doubles tournaments

Session 13

- Team competitions

Appendix:
Basic Simplified Badminton Rules

This appendix introduces basic badminton rules. Rules that are practical for regular badminton classes are introduced in a simplified way so that students will understand and remember these rules easily. Comprehensive badminton rules can be found on the International Badminton Federation and USA Badminton websites.

Equipment and Facility

Lines and Courts

Six different lines are on the badminton court. Combinations of these lines make a singles court for singles games or a doubles court for doubles games.

- Singles court: after the service, the shaded area is the full court for singles games (the shaded area in Figure A-1).
- Doubles court: after the service, the shaded area is the full court for doubles games (the shaded area in Figure A-2).
- Court lines (functions) (Figure A-3):
    ✓ Doubles sideline (#1)—for doubles games only

    ✓ Singles sideline (#2)—for singles games

    ✓ Center line (#3)—for singles and doubles service

    ✓ Back boundary line (#4)—for singles serves and shots and double shots

    ✓ Back service line for doubles (#5)—long service line for doubles

    ✓ Front service line (#6)—for singles and doubles service
- Singles and doubles service area: when starting each inning (i.e., term of service), both the player and the receiver should remain in their designated areas. A serve that is out-of-bounds is a fault serve, and the server loses the serve. The server must remain in his position on one side of the court (left or right) and serve diagonally (across the court) to the receiver's receiving area. The server's area and the receiver's area are the same except that they are on opposite sides of the court. Lines 3, 5, and 6 are for service only. After the server delivers the serve, these lines do not exist anymore during the rally until the next serve. The singles service area (Figure A-4) is narrow and long, while the doubles service area (Figure A-5) is wide and short.

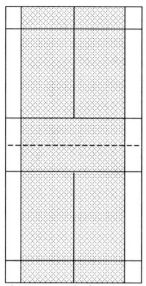

Figure A-1. Singles court

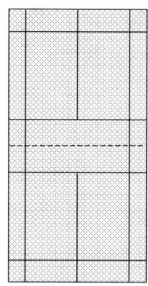

Figure A-2. Doubles court

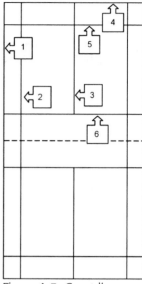

Figure A-3. Court lines

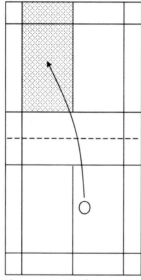

Figure A-4. Singles service area

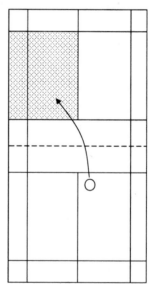

Figure A-5. Doubles service area

Net and Post

- Net width, 7.6 centimeters
- Net height, 152.4 centimeters (5 feet) in the middle and 155 centimeters (5 feet 1 inch) at the post
- Pole height, 155 centimeters (5 feet 1 inch)

Shuttlecocks

- Nylon (similar to feather birds; Figure 2-5):
    - ✓ Usually for high school games and practice
    - ✓ Also used for university classes
- Feather (Figure 2-6):
    - ✓ 16 feathers, 6.4 to 7 centimeters long
    - ✓ Form a diameter, 5.8 to 6.8 centimeters
    - ✓ Base, 2.5 to 2.8 centimeters in diameter
    - ✓ Weight, 4.74 to 5.5 grams
    - ✓ For high-level competitions and community play
- Testing shuttlecocks: make an underhand clear serve at the back boundary line; the bird should land within 53 to 99 centimeters from the other back boundary line.

Rackets

- Rackets should not exceed 68 centimeters in overall length and 23 centimeters in overall width.
- The strung surface should not exceed 28 centimeters in overall length and 220 centimeters in overall width.

Game Patterns

Following are the five basic game patterns in badminton competitions, including both individual competitions and team competitions, in all tournaments:

- Men's singles game (one man vs. one man) using the singles court.
- Women's singles game (one woman vs. one woman) using the singles court.
- Men's doubles game (two men vs. two men) using the doubles court.
- Women's doubles game (two women vs. two women) using the doubles court.
- Mixed doubles game (a man and a woman as a team vs. another combination of a man and a woman) using the doubles court.

Scoring

All games (men's, women's, singles, and doubles) play up to 21 points. One side must lead by at least two points to win the game (e.g., 21 to 19 or 21 to 16). If no side leads by two points after both sides reach 20 points or more, then the side who reaches 30 points first wins the game, no matter how many points the opponent has (even up to 29 points).

The player who wins an inning wins a point, no matter if that player is serving or receiving. The winner of an inning keeps serving until that player loses the serve.

Games and Matches

Games

When a side gets 21 points and leads by two points (or reaches 30 points first) in any of the five games, this side wins the game. Then, the players switch ends and start the second game. The winner of the first game serves first in the second game.

Matches

In most tournaments, players must win two of three games to win a match: if team (or player) A wins the first two games, the match is over; however, if teams A and B tie at one game each, then a third game must be played. The rules for the third game are the same as those for the previous games except the two teams change ends when a team (or player) reaches 11 points. The player who was serving before changing ends continues serving.

Service Order

Singles Game Serving Rotation

In singles games, the server serves from the right side if the server's score is even and from the left side if the server's score is odd. The receiver just follows the server and takes a diagonal position. The server serves diagonally to the receiver.

Doubles Game Serving Rotation

In doubles, if the serving side's score is even, then the player on the right side serves. If the serving side's score is odd, then the player on the left side serves. When the server scores, he switches to the other side (left or right) and serves to the other opponent. When the server loses the inning, the serve goes to the opponent directly without the second player serving.

Toss and Choices

A toss is usually used to determine which side serves first in the first game and who picks the side. The toss can be performed with a coin (choose heads or tails and then flip the coin to see how it lands; the winner of the toss chooses first) or a shuttlecock (hit a shuttlecock up high in the air and watch it land; the person the bottom points toward is the winner of the toss and chooses first).

The winner of the toss can choose the side (end) or to serve first or not to serve first. The loser of the toss must take one of the remaining choices. If the winner picks the side (end), then the loser should choose to serve. If the winner wants to serve first, then the loser must pick the side (end).

Changing Ends

- Both players (or sides in doubles) should change ends after each game.
- During the third game, when a player (or sides in doubles) reaches 11 points first, both players (or sides in doubles games) should change ends.

Shuttlecock Not in Play

Following are situations during which the shuttlecock is not in play (players should not hit the shuttlecock in these situations):
- Before the server is ready to serve.
- The shuttlecock hits the net and remains there.
- The shuttlecock hits any player's body.
- The shuttlecock hits the surface of the floor.
- A fault or let has occurred.

Legal Shots

Following are legal shots that should be returned by opponents (if an opponent returns the shot, then the game continues; if the shot is not returned, the hitter wins the rally):
- Hitting the bird before it touches the floor.
- Hitting the bird over the net.
- Hitting the bird into the opponent's court.

Faults in Play

Following are situations in which a fault is called (the player who hits or is supposed to hit the shuttlecock loses the rally):
- The shuttlecock lands outside of the court.
- The shuttlecock fails to pass over the net.
- The shuttlecock passes through or under the net.
- The player fails to return the bird to the opponent's side.
- The player hits the shuttlecock twice in singles; one player hits the shuttlecock and then the partner hits it again in doubles.

- The racket contacts the shuttlecock on the opponent's side.
- The receiver's partner returns a serve that should be returned by the receiver.
- The player carries the shuttlecock over the net instead of hitting it.
- The player (his racket, body, or clothing) touches the net when the bird is still in play (the shot is not dead yet).
- The player's racket or body invades the opponent's court.
- The player tries to prevent an opponent from making a legal shot near the net (such as using the racket to block an opponent's racket).
- The player deliberately distracts an opponent.
- The player conducts repeated or persistent offenses.

Service Court Errors

A service court error means a player has served out-of-turn, has served from the wrong service court, or is standing in the wrong service court and is prepared to receive a serve. When a service court error has been made, the following occurs:

- It is called a let if the error is discovered before the next serve unless one side loses the rally.
- The point is replayed when a let is called.

Legal Serves

Following are the key elements of legal serves (the receiver should return these services; otherwise, he loses a point):

- Both server and receiver stand diagonally in designated courts without touching any line; both feet or parts of both feet are on the floor, with no movement at the moment of service.
- The racket hits the base of the shuttlecock.
- The racket head must be lower than the serving hand and the lowest rib at the moment of service; usually, the racket is pointed upward at about 45 degrees.
- The first forward swing indicates the start of a serve, and the motion should be continuous.
- After hitting the shuttlecock, the bird should fly over the net toward the opponent's court.
- The server should not serve before the receiver is ready, and the receiver should not return a serve if he is not ready; however, the game continues if the receiver returns the serve.
- The game continues when the receiver returns the serve no matter if the serve is short, long, or out-of-bounds.

- In doubles games, the server's partner may take any position as long as he does not block the view of the serve.
- The server wins a point when the receiver fails to return the serve or shot or makes a fault.
- The server loses the serve when he fails to serve over or makes a fault; the receiver gets the serve and a point.
- Either player of the winning side in doubles games may serve first in the next game, and either player of the losing side may receive first.

Faults in Serves

Following are situations in which the server loses the serve (then, the opponent gets the serve and a point).
- The server delays the serve on purpose.
- The server moves a foot (or feet) at the moment of delivery of the serve.
- The server uses fake motions.
- The server misses the bird.
- The bird is caught on the net after passing over the net.
- The bird lands out-of-bounds.
- The bird fails to pass over the net.
- The bird passes through or under the net.
- The bird touches the ceiling, wall, pole, or any object outside of the court.
- The bird lands in a wrong court in service.
- The bird is higher than the serving hand, racket head, or lowest rib.

Let: Replay the Point

Following are situations in which a let is called (then, the server reserves the point):
- Any unforeseen accidental occurrence.
- A shuttlecock passes over the net and is caught on the net except in service.
- The server and receiver both have service faults.
- The server serves before the receiver is ready.
- The bird falls apart during the game.
- The side making calls is not sure if a shot (serve) is in or out.

About the Authors

Dr. Gong Chen is a professor in the Department of Kinesiology at San Jose State University. Dr. Chen teaches all levels of badminton classes at San Jose State University and coaches the San Jose State University badminton club, which has won many collegiate championships in Northern California. Dr. Chen has directed and been an instructor at San Jose State University badminton summer camps since 2001. In addition, he was an instructor at a 2002 camp with Dr. Li Lingwei, a 13-time world champion. Dr. Chen has also organized many badminton tournaments at San Jose State University.

Carol Chen is an assistant coach at Lynbrook High School (San Jose, CA). She is a student of Dr. Li Lingwei, coach Yuan Wang, and coach Cania Zhang. Chen played on Lynbrook High School's badminton team and won many tournament titles in women's singles and doubles. She was a Central Coast Section player.